Searching for a Pastor
the Presbyterian Way

Searching for a Pastor
the Presbyterian Way

A Roadmap for Pastor
Nominating Committees

Dean E. Foose

Geneva Press
Louisville, Kentucky

© 2001 by Dean E. Foose

Book design by Sharon Adams

First edition
Published by Geneva Press
Louisville, Kentucky

This book is printed on acid-free paper that meets the American National Standards Institute Z39.48 standard. ♾

PRINTED IN THE UNITED STATES OF AMERICA

08 09 10 — 10 9 8

Library of Congress Cataloging-in-Publication Data

Foose, Dean E.
    Searching for a pastor the Presbyterian way / Dean E. Foose.
        p. cm.
    Includes bibliographical references.
    ISBN-13: 978-0-664-50041-2 (pbk.)
    ISBN-10: 0-664-50041-2 (pbk.)
    1. Presbyterian Church—Clergy—Appointment, call, and
    election. I. Title.
BX9195.F66 2000
253—dc21   00-041716

Contents

Preface

*C*ongratulations! You are about to begin a remark-able adventure—the search for new leadership for your congregation. It is likely that this book is in your hands because your congregation has elected you to serve on a pastor nominating committee (PNC) or an associate pastor nominating committee (APNC). Your election was an official action, but, more deeply, it was an act of trust on the part of your congregation. Eventually you will nominate a can-didate for pastor or associate pastor of your congre-gation, and the congregation will vote to extend a call. In the meantime, the members of your congre-gation have entrusted you to do the work the whole congregation cannot do: to search for a fitting candidate.

Calling new pastoral leadership is essentially a theological task, a work of spiritual discernment. Your work in determining your congregation's needs and in seeking for suitable pastoral leadership can deepen and enrich your faith, and many people have reported that serving on a search committee is a life-changing experience. The task not only deepened their faith but also expanded their understanding of the church and the mission of Christ. You have a

challenging responsibility before you, and it is my hope
that the information and examples offered in these pages
will serve as a helpful guide as you move into this adventure and begin your search.

I am a Presbyterian minister, and I served both as an
assistant pastor and as a pastor for a total of twenty-two
years, in three different congregations. In that time, I esti-
mate that, as I considered new calls, I talked in depth with
about twenty committees such as yours and I exchanged
information with probably twenty or more others.
Although years have passed since those interviews and
exchanges of information, I still remember many of the
committees, the individuals who served on them, and the
conversations I had. I came to know the faith experiences
and ministry visions of a wide range of congregations.
Undoubtedly you, too, will remember candidates and
conversations long after your search work has been completed, and throughout your search you will come to know
the breadth and depth of faith of a variety of candidates.

I am currently the director of alumni/ae relations and
placement at Princeton Theological Seminary. Since part
of my ministry is to serve as something of a broker
between churches and pastors, I now view the search
process from a different perspective. I work with seniors
as they prepare and polish their Personal Information
Forms (PIFs) and ready themselves for interviews for
their first positions in pastoral ministry. I also work with
experienced pastors and associate pastors who have
served many years in the church and who are now seeking new challenges. In addition, I consult with nominating committees from congregations seeking pastors and
associate pastors. I see search processes that go smoothly
and well, and I also see committees stumble unnecessar-
ily, with needless breakdowns in communication between
ministers and committees.

A number of books have been written about the calling of new pastoral leadership, and many of them contain valuable insights. None of them, however, specifically addresses the *Presbyterian* process of calling pastors, the process that you are about to begin. Therefore, after years of observing the Presbyterian way of searching for a pastor, I decided to write this book, based on what I have learned watching many search committees go about their work, and on my own experiences and discoveries as a pastor and now an adviser to ministers and congregations.

I have been humbled by this task. Early in my research, I thought about trying to write a comprehensive manual for the search process, but then I read in my old *Webster's Third New International Dictionary* the dictionary definition of the word "manual": "a book containing in concise form the principles, rules, and directions needed for the mastery of an art, science, or skill." I changed my mind. The process of calling pastors is, to be sure, "an art, science, or skill," but who can put together "in concise form the principles, rules, and directions needed for mastery" of this complex and variable task?

Consequently the aim of this book is more modest. I would describe it as an overview or a road map, a general guide to follow as you progress through the work of calling pastoral leadership. If you examine the contents page, you will find outlined the basic steps you will take, but your committee will need to modify and adapt these steps to make them your own. Perhaps before developing a plan of action you will want to get a broad sense of the process by briefly reviewing the whole book. Then you can go back and read it more closely and carefully.

Throughout your search you will need to be flexible and creative. There is no one "right way." There are no formulas or recipes to follow that will guarantee success. This responsibility will take time, a sense of humor, large doses of wisdom, and lots of energy, commitment, patience, ingenuity, imagination, love, hope, and faith.

Acknowledgments

I appreciate the help of the following people:

Tom Long, who said, "You ought to write a book that would help search committees with their work," and who made it possible for this book to be published.

Houston Hodges and Ray Trout, who helped get the project going.

Zane Brown, John Gmitro, John Laffety, Rosemary Mace, Mary McKey, and Janet Walker, who all provided me with both materials from their PNCs and APNCs and fine counsel on how their search committees went about their work.

Barbara Chaapel and Bob MacLennan, who helped me refine the content of this book.

My wife, Sandy Foose, who has written nine books and who continually said to me, "Sure it's hard work, but it will be worth the effort."

Lori Cummings and Esther Kolb, project editor and copy editor, who put the final polish on this book.

Chapter 1

What Lies Ahead?

As you engage in a search for new pastoral leadership, be prepared to make some gratifying spiritual discoveries. For many of you, this experience will be like sailing in uncharted waters or taking a boat down a river you have never traveled. In all waters there are some unexpected challenges: shoals, logjams, swift currents, high winds that come up quickly out of nowhere and make waves that rock the boat. That's all right. We all know that life isn't always smooth sailing. Take heart. There are also deep currents of joy, breathtaking scenery, and a profound sense of being carried by the wind of the Spirit. You are not in these waters by yourself. The New Testament is full of stories about Jesus carefully choosing leaders for his new community, and Christ, as Lord of the church, travels with you in your adventure of choosing leadership.

Still, one myth needs to be challenged right at the beginning of the journey, namely, the idea that God is a "heavenly matchmaker." Some members of search committees think that God has in mind one, and only one, person for their church—a "Rev. Mr. or Ms. Perfect"—and that it is the committee's job simply to follow God's leading to this already divinely anointed person. Theologically speaking, though, there is no such thing as a pastoral match made *purely* in heaven. Presbyterians believe that God gives us great freedom to make decisions in the church, and finding good leadership for your church is a combination of prayerfully seeking God's guidance and the hard, earthly work of diligent, faithful people using their God-given abilities and skills in a work of spiritual discernment.

In his book *In Search of a Leader,* Robert Dingman challenges the idea that God has in mind only one person for every position of ministry. Dingman, a Presbyterian and the son of a minister, heads his own executive search firm and has over thirty years' experience as an executive recruiter. He recognizes that every search committee naturally hopes to find a leader whose ministry is blessed by God, and this is good. But this hope sometimes leads people to believe that God has somehow preselected a specific person to be their leader, that if they somehow miss finding "God's perfect will" for them in this matter, they are sure to have less than the best that God planned for them. But is this a scriptural position? No, argues Dingman. He quotes Haddon Robinson, president of Denver Seminary, to the effect that the Bible provides much guidance about church leadership and that the principles and guidelines in the Bible allow for the possibility of a number of acceptable candidates, not just one. God doesn't do the decision making, but gives us wisdom in the Bible for the search and then entrusts the task to us.

I agree. I receive a number of letters from pastor nominating committees asking for assistance in finding "the person God has in mind" as their new pastor. But what does this mean theologically if "the person God has in mind" does not feel called to this church, or perhaps does come to the church but then finds the pastoral relationship doesn't work out? Do we blame God for this failure? I don't think God has only one person in mind for each pastoral position in the Presbyterian Church (U.S.A.). Spiritual discernment does not mean knowing precisely the person God has in mind. Rather, it is a combination of prayer and perseverance, employing every gift and skill God has given us to identify the best pool of pastoral candidates, then asking God to guide us in the hard work of discerning who should be called to this place of ministry.

What Makes for Effective Pastoral Leadership?

Most Presbyterian churches, like many congregations in other denominations, have changed dramatically over the last few decades, and, as a result, the role of pastoral leaders has changed as well. The old joke about ministers "working only one day a week" was never true, and it is certainly not true now. Even smaller churches usually have a wide array of programs, activities, and pastoral needs, and regardless of whether ministers want it or welcome it, the role of the pastor has greatly expanded. Being a pastor today often means being a combination of worship leader, preacher, administrator, teacher, counselor, social worker, small-group facilitator, community advocate, and spiritual guide. Every pastor takes on these various roles through a particular leadership style, and that style is determined by three basic factors: the gifts and skills of the leader, the people in the congregation and their expectations, and the tasks that must be accomplished. Indeed, a key issue you will grapple with in your search is the specific type of leadership your congregation needs. You must focus on what that leadership would look like as your congregation experiences it. One style of leadership doesn't fit all congregations.

Congregations usually expect a great deal from ministers, sometimes too much, almost perfection. Congregations realize that pastors are the pacesetters for the ministry of the whole church and that it is difficult for a community of faith to change or develop without the support and cooperation of the pastor. Consequently, search committees usually seek leaders who have produced results in other settings. We need to realize, though, that good pastoral leadership doesn't always provide immediate results or success. Ministry is a seed-planting business, and sometimes the harvest is seen only later (this can be frustrating for pastors, since the service they offer is often so intangible). We should also recognize that ministry today takes place in an environment of much more fragile trust. People don't give trust and authority to ministers as quickly or easily as they once did. This shouldn't surprise us, since the same thing is true of institutional leadership in all other areas of society too. Presidents and other politicians, business leaders, physicians, lawyers, and representatives of the news media are no longer granted automatic authority and trust, and the same is true for the clergy.

The qualities that make for an effective pastor are very difficult to name, much less to measure. Indeed, it is so difficult to say what makes for an able pastor that the church has, unfortunately, too often taken the easy way out and gauged pastors by the standards of the world: more, more, more—more people, more money, more buildings, more programs. To be sure, helping a church to grow can be an indication of pastoral gifts and the ability to lead, but there are other important standards of leadership we should use as well.

How can we get a handle on what constitutes quality pastoral leadership? First, we should remember the biblical counsel concerning leadership, and a good place to begin is by reading 1 and 2 Timothy. There a pastor called a "bishop" (or more literally, an "overseer") is described as someone who is above reproach, temperate, sensible, respectable, hospitable, an apt teacher, and gentle. We are also reminded in those letters that administration is not a necessary evil but a spiritual task in the church, and that the task of preaching demands hard work and discipline. Explore also the biblical stories that tell how God calls people to daring service. Read the stories of Abraham and Sarah, Moses and Miriam, Deborah, David, and Daniel, Mary and Martha, Peter and Andrew, and a host of others.

In addition to the biblical witness, we can also learn from the experience and wisdom of proven pastoral leaders. William Hobgood, a regional minister of the Christian Church (Disciples of Christ) in the Washington, D.C., area and a seasoned pastor, interviewed thirty-two pastors who led congregations that experienced a renewal in vitality and faith, meaningful growth, and spiritual excitement. From his conversations with these pastors, seven qualities of effective pastoral leadership became clear:

1. Effective pastors are *spiritually grounded.* Hobgood suggests they are so dependent on the spirit of God that they repeatedly go to God for insight, inspiration, strength, and rest, and each realizes he or she can't do anything in ministry without these qualities.

2. Effective pastors are *trusted and trusting.* Hobgood discovered that to be trusted, a pastor must trust. He found trusted pastors don't form cliques or special alliances. Trusted pastors don't violate others' trust. Trusted and trusting pastors reveal a transparent integrity. They don't have to tell people, "I am your leader."

3. Effective pastors are *committed to a future of hope.* These are pastors who are not satisfied with maintaining the status quo. They are vision-casting and vision-catching leaders. Their leadership gives direction and purpose and meaning.

4. Effective pastors are *mission-focused*. Mission-focused leadership is the way a pastor helps a congregation understand and describe the future to which they are committed.

5. Effective pastors are *committed to shared leadership*. Hobgood notes that shared leadership is trusted and trusting leadership. Pastors who share leadership work collaboratively. They draw on gifts, talents, and insights from a host of others.

6. Effective pastors are *committed to truth telling*. These pastors genuinely struggle with the truth and its fallout. Hobgood points out that if a pastor says one thing and does another, makes promises with no apparent intention of keeping them, avoids grappling with her or his own deepest dilemmas, refuses to hear and accept feedback, preaches and teaches pabulum instead of solid food, always takes the focus away from the other person and brings it to the self, then truth telling is not present.

7. Effective pastors are *attuned to the world*. They read with the Bible in one hand and the newspaper in the other. Effective pastors know they need to be aware of what is going on in the world around them. They work at knowing and understanding public life. They read a variety of journals. They equip their congregations to interact with systems outside the congregation: the local neighborhood, the larger community, town, or city, and institutions such as the media, schools, and other communities of faith, Christian and non-Christian.

Edward White, another seasoned pastor, executive presbyter, and now a consultant for the Alban Institute, adds another perspective on pastoral leadership. In an article in *Congregations* titled "What Kind of Pastor Will Most Likely Empower Laity?" he offers six vital qualities of good pastoral leadership:

1. Pastors who empower laity, and thus the whole church, are those pastors who are secure in their sense of self. They are not threatened by those people who seem bigger or smarter or stronger than they are. One sign of spiritual maturity is that a pastor is secure enough to help others become more accomplished than he or she is.

2. Pastors who can empower laity, White goes on to say, can also clearly define themselves. Such pastors can state clearly where they stand and why, without being judgmental. They speak with inward authority and do not worry about external control.

3. Empowering pastors are grounded in the midst of ambiguity and conflict. They don't convey anxiety, but instead have an inner peace. They remain connected to members of their congregations in nonanxious ways as their people struggle with issues, often in heated and anxiety-producing confrontations.

4. Empowering pastors are clear about their own possibilities and limitations. White believes pastors who empower laity live out of the famous "serenity prayer": "God, grant me the courage to change what can be changed, the serenity to accept what cannot be changed, and the wisdom to know the one from the other."

5. Empowering pastors practice solidarity. They don't need someone else to lose in order for them to win. They carry the banner of collaboration in a society that is compulsively competitive.

6. Last but not least in his list, White says pastors who empower laity are also free from the constraints of careerism and consumerism: more money, more people, more buildings, more programs. They don't live by a compulsive workaholism, which conveys a message of justification by works. They preach and live justification by God's grace.

Other Resources

I have listed a number of books on pastoral leadership in the Bibliography, and I urge you to become acquainted with as many as you can. A good review of how the dramatic change in our culture has affected the church is William Hobgood's *The Once and Future Pastor.* His chapter "Tomorrow's Shepherds" spells out in detail his seven qualities of effective pastors. Edward White's "What Kind of Pastor Will Most Likely Empower Laity?" is very brief and fleshes out his perspective on pastoral leadership. Danny Morris and Charles Olsen coauthored *Discerning God's Will Together: A Spiritual Practice for the Church,* which in my judgment presents the most thorough treatment of the subject of spiritual discernment. In their book *The Equipping Pastor: A Systems Approach to Congregational Leadership,* R. Paul Stevens and Phil Collins devote an insightful chapter to "Matching Leadership Styles." They note that there is no biblical or theological support for one style of leadership over another. Bunty Ketchum, a consultant in organizational development specializing in helping organizations and individuals face major transitions, has written a brief but very readable book, *So You're on the Search Committee,* based on an interview that Celia Hahn, a former editor with Alban Institute, conducted with her. The book has much wisdom for a search committee to consider, compacted into twenty-four pages. Robert Dingman's book *In Search of a Leader* has a wealth of helpful insight for search committees. The cartoons alone are worth the price of the book.

Understanding the Alphabet: PNC/APNC, COM, CIF, PIF, CPM

I use a number of abbreviations in this book, some of which you will know. Others may be new and unfamiliar.

Here are some aids.

PNC/APNC	Pastor nominating committee or associate pastor nominating committee
COM	Committee on ministry, a committee of your presbytery and every other presbytery that has responsibility for pastors and congregations
CPM	Committee on preparation for ministry, a presbytery committee with the special responsibility for the care and oversight of Presbyterians preparing for ordained ministry of Word and sacrament
CRS	Call Referral Services, the Louisville office that will assist you in your work
CIF	Church Information Form, the document or material you will prepare and use as your congregation's "résumé" or profile
PIF	Personal Information Form, the document or material pastors and candidates use as their "résumé" or profile

In short order these abbreviations will be as familiar to you as PTA/PTO, CIA, or UFO.

The Bottom Line: Trust

One more word before we proceed. You are looking for pastoral leadership that is effective. Pastors want to be in a place where they can express their deepest passion for ministry, best use their gifts and skills, and be challenged to grow. I believe if attention is given to key ingredients in the search process by search teams and pastors, mismatches can be avoided and "calls" can become a better fit. The bottom line is building trust.

Chapter 2

"Decently and in Order"

*Calling Pastoral Leadership
the Presbyterian Way*

"Seemliness and Peace"

Presbyterians long ago decided that Paul's advice
to the church in Corinth, "All things should be done
decently and in order" (1 Corinthians 14:40), was
good basic counsel. What did Paul mean by this
phrase? John Calvin, the sixteenth-century Swiss
reformer and one of the pioneers of Reformed theology and the Presbyterian form of government, suggests that Paul was describing how the Corinthians
should receive the instructions that Paul himself was
giving the congregation. By telling the church how
to proceed in certain circumstances, Paul was not
trying to bind the conscience of his readers, observed
Calvin. He did not want the Corinthians to receive
his instructions as rules that had to be obeyed simply
for the sake of obedience. Rather, they were to weigh
his words, consider his instructions, and follow them
only insofar as they made for "seemliness and
peace." For Calvin, this principle of "seemliness and
peace," or "decency and order," names a worthy goal
toward which the church should strive when it deals
with difficult situations.

It is no wonder that the Scots Confession, a creed
of our forebears written in 1560 after a season of

bloodshed and acrimonious conflict in the church, also places great value on the phrase "decently and in order." Whenever the church faces volatile and potentially controversial issues, we Presbyterians have been eager to lift up the banner of peace by reminding ourselves of the wisdom to "let all things be done decently and in order."

There is real merit in applying these words to the task of calling new pastors. There is a "Presbyterian" way to follow, but this way is not a set of rigid rules or a specific template that will fit each congregation. We are to consider the instructions thoughtfully and follow them only insofar as they make for "seemliness and peace." Presbyterians have long been thoughtful people, given to reflection, discussion, and debate (after all, our system of church government was the pattern used to shape our nation's government!). Presbyterians know that seeking new pastoral leadership sometimes takes us into controversial places and that people will often disagree about important matters. In the Presbyterian way of calling pastoral leaders, discussion, debate, even disagreements are fine as long as we remember to do things "decently and in order," allowing the process to be one of spiritual discernment and decision making guided by prayer.

How Long, O Lord?

How long will your work take? Maybe nine months, maybe two-plus years. But be careful about setting a specific time line, and don't set a rigid calendar to follow; you might think you are bogged down in the process if your time line doesn't work according to the plan you set. Searching for effective pastoral leadership can take some time. Most likely you will be meeting once a week for two hours. I tell seminary seniors that the search process involves a lot of people, a lot of paper, a lot of prayer, and a lot of patience. Indeed, I have a chorus that I will sing throughout this book: *Don't rush the process.* Another word of counsel is equally important, however: *Don't get bogged down in the process.* Prayer will be crucial for your work—your prayers and others' prayers for you. There may be times of discouragement. Therefore, patience will also be crucial.

In the Beginning

At the beginning of your search process, recognize the biblical and theological foundation for our status as people of God. We are a product of God's persistent work of calling and shaping a faithful people. Our Presbyterian system of government calls for continuity with and faithfulness to the heritage that lies behind the contemporary church. It calls equally for openness and faithfulness to the renewing activity of the God of history.

You are connected to an ancient heritage. God has been calling leaders since the beginning of history: people such as Abraham, Sarah, Moses, Miriam, David, Peter, Andrew, Mary, Martha, Priscilla, and Paul, to name just a few. You don't have to read much beyond the calling of Abraham and Sarah in the Bible to see that calling leadership is hard work. "Time would fail me to tell of Gideon, Barak, Samson, Jephthah, of David and Samuel and the prophets—who through faith conquered kingdoms, administered justice, obtained promises, shut the mouths of lions, quenched raging fire, escaped the edge of the sword, won strength out of weakness" (Hebrews 11:32–34). You are surrounded by a great cloud of witnesses, as the writer of the book of Hebrews claims. You are not only connected to this ancient heritage: you are an instrument of God continuing the heritage.

These numerous accounts of God at work building a

community of faith through people such as Sarah and Abraham and all the matriarchs and patriarchs are not only your heritage, but are instructive for you in calling new pastoral leadership. These accounts should remind you that God has not often had it easy in the leadership department. Finding effective leaders has at times been hard. The accounts of Jesus' calls to his disciples, and of the Spirit at work through Paul's and others' letters, are good counsel for you. Jesus reminded his disciples about the renewing work of God in history. "The Advocate, the Holy Spirit, whom the Father will send in my name, will teach you everything, and remind you of all that I have said to you" (John 14:26).

Presbyterians have a firm theological foundation, and we have written it into our Form of Government. We believe "God has put all things under the Lordship of Jesus Christ and has made Christ Head of the Church, which is his body. Christ calls the church into being, giving it all that is necessary for its mission to the world, for its building up, and for its service to God. Christ is present with the church in both Spirit and Word. It belongs to Christ alone to rule, to teach, to call, and to use the Church as he wills, exercising his authority by the ministry of women and men for the establishment and extension of his Kingdom."

Presbyterians have always had a strong conviction that Jesus, the Lord of the church, is keenly interested in the kind of leadership we have in his church. He shows this interest again and again in the Gospels. He goes to the Sea of Galilee and recruits fishermen accustomed to hard work to be leaders. He also selects a tax collector, a skeptic, and a zealot. He says to all of his disciples, "You know that among the Gentiles those whom they recognize as their rulers lord it over them, and their great ones are tyrants over them. But it is not so among you; but whoever wishes to become great among you must be your servant" (Mark 10:42–43).

Finding a Pastor the Presbyterian Way: A Committee

If it's the "Presbyterian way," you can bet that a committee will be involved. We have learned that committees are a way of doing things decently and in order. When a Presbyterian church gets ready to call new leadership, the entire congregation elects a pastor nominating committee (PNC) or associate pastor nominating committee (APNC) at a meeting called specifically for that purpose. The congregation then entrusts the committee to do the discernment work of finding a candidate. While your committee will do the bulk of the work of seeking new pastoral leadership, the attitude and understanding most helpful to develop in your congregation is "*We* are in this together; *we* are calling a new pastor." Some people don't like the word "committee," so, if you prefer, think of your group as a team. A number of churches refer to all their committees as "ministry teams." I will use both terms throughout this book.

No matter what name you go by, there is a job to do, and you have been elected to do it. You will be reporting your progress to the congregation from time to time, but you will work confidentially. The end result of your work will be finding a candidate to nominate and present to the congregation. The congregation, by a vote, will extend a call. You are an extension of the congregation, and you represent it, to the best of your ability.

Making Your Committee Effective

People

The most important factors in the effectiveness of a search committee are the people who make up the membership and the attitude they bring to their service. Good people come from across the spectrum of work and vocation: teachers, doctors, farmers, homemakers, cabinet-makers, lawyers, people from industry and business, people who may be unemployed or retired. One organizational consultant who consults frequently with search committees, Bunty Ketchum, offers several insights on committee members and their work. She writes that effective committee members are people who are known for their genuine concern for the whole church, and for their good judgment. They are able to work well as group members; that is, they respect others' ideas and are not overly outspoken, opinionated, or divisive. They are objective and fair and able to represent the whole congregation in a professional way. Patience is very important in an effective committee—patience with the process and with one another. Keeping a positive attitude is essential and makes the process much more pleasurable. The congregation will pick up this attitude and reflect it in their patience, their outlook, and their satisfaction with what happens. If your committee remains positive and patient, the congregation will also be more excited and supportive when your nomination is made, since they will feel the energy, excitement, and satisfaction of the committee in its work.

Size

Should the committee be large or small? There are trade-offs. I prefer a smaller committee, seven to eleven members, as a smaller group often provides the environment for a free exchange of opinion during meetings. However, larger committees have advantages as well. A larger committee may represent more groups in the congregation, and more of the needed skills for an effective search may be included in a larger group. Then too, a larger team can be divided into smaller working units in order to accomplish the sizable amount of work required in a search process. The sharing of perspectives, apprehensions, expectations, and hopes so vital in the search process will take more time in a larger committee. A high degree of discipline is especially vital in a larger committee. Such discipline results from a combination of firm leadership from the chair and self-control on the part of the other members.

A Little Help from Your Friends

The Presbyterian way for finding a leader is not perfect, of course, but it is effective. One of the best features of the Presbyterian way is that your committee will be traveling a well-marked path and will have some experienced companions to accompany you on your way. There are official constitutional procedures to follow (see Appendix A), and your presbytery, through its committee on ministry (COM), will give your congregation guidance. If your presbytery provides training sessions for PNCs/APNCs, I recommend that you take advantage of them.

Sometimes committees are puzzled by presbytery's involvement, and may even bristle a bit, because they see it as overly cumbersome or as an intrusion into the affairs of the local congregation. Why should your presbytery become involved in your search for a leader? Why should it look over your shoulder in the process? Actually, there are several good reasons for presbytery to be involved. First, the whole Presbyterian Church cares who your pastor or associate pastor will be and has a vital stake in your finding a good leader. If your church has healthy leadership, the larger church is stronger for it. Indeed, calls to pastors and associate pastors must be approved by presbytery, and this process will usually go much more smoothly when presbytery is a part of the process from the beginning. Second, many members of presbytery have deep experience guiding congregations in the search process, and they can bring that wisdom to your work. Third, the presbytery often has access to information not readily available to a local committee. For example, the presbytery may become aware of capable ministers who are open to a new position, or may know of problems in a candidate's background not revealed to the committee.

The COM oversees the relationships between all pastors in the presbytery and their congregations. It has some of the responsibilities and some of the powers that bishops have in other denominations. It is charged with oversight of the search process for new pastoral leadership and will work closely with you. Ordinarily, each church seeking new pastoral leadership will have a liaison representing the COM of its presbytery. Good COMs can keep a search committee from getting into trouble.

Some COM procedures vary from presbytery to presbytery, such as the manner of *how* counsel and advice is given and how *frequently* counsel and advice will be given. Each presbytery puts together guidelines based on its interpretation of a specific section of the *Book of Order* dealing with the responsibilities of the committee on ministry of the presbytery, and I have listed that section in Appendix A, G-11.0502.

When the liaison or representative from the COM first meets with your search committee, you should get specific answers to at least two questions: (1) What will the COM require of your committee concerning a mission study? and (2) How will the COM perform its *Book of Order* responsibilities, namely, to "advise [you] regarding the merits, availability, and suitability of any candidate or minister whose name is contemplated for nomination to the congregation" and to exercise the "privilege of suggesting names to the committee"? Find out if your COM plans to review all candidates or ministers you consider or just the one you plan to nominate to the congregation.

Candidates just graduating from seminary or recently graduated and not yet ordained are under the care of a specific presbytery's committee on preparation for ministry (CPM). Sometimes when a PNC or APNC is considering a candidate not yet ordained, the COM of the PNC or APNC's presbytery will need to talk with the candidate's CPM. There are occasions when a COM in one presbytery will disagree with a ruling of a CPM in another presbytery or vice versa, and a congregation seeking to call a new pastor or associate pastor gets caught in the middle of the debate. If this happens to you, be patient and prayerful. Remember, "all things . . . decently and in order." These debates are usually for good reason and have good results.

Family Systems and Ghostbusters

If your congregation is like most, be ready during the search process for some "ghosts" to come out of the closet or down from the attic or up from the cellar. Ghosts can be feelings about previous pastors or previous members. Ghosts can be old church fights or a building campaign that came up short of the goal.

Ghosts come out because congregations are systems that operate much like families. A congregation is a community made up of individuals, but the operative word here is *community*. To paraphrase Aristotle, a congregation is more than the sum of its individual members. We may think we are independent people, both in our families and in our congregations, but actually we are interdependent. We are tied together in family and in congregations like the parts of a mobile; changes in one "arm" produce change in all the others. Paul knew this when he said to the divided church at Corinth: "If the foot would say, 'Because I am not a hand, I do not belong to the body,' that would not make it any less a part of the body. . . . If the whole body were an eye, where would the hearing be? If the whole body were hearing, where would the sense of smell be?" (1 Corinthians 12:15–17).

Church folk haven't changed much since Paul's time. Congregations still quarrel and divide for a host of reasons. Emotions can run high where guilt feelings and the pressure to get along sometimes push problems beneath the surface, allowing them to fester for years. Congregations can be wounded, hurt, bruised, and in need of healing.

What are some of the ghosts that can emerge? Sometimes a previous pastor has died unexpectedly, leaving a congregation in unresolved grief. Numerous pastoral relationships have been dissolved because of sexual misconduct on the part of pastors, leaving angry, hurt, frustrated congregations in the wake. Unhappy memories may linger in the air when there has been a mismatch between the leadership style of a previous pastor and what a congregation expected. There are congregations that thought they were calling a strong leader, and the person turned out to be a tyrant. There are congregations that thought they were calling a gentle, warmhearted pastor to guide them, and the person turned out to have no heart for ministry and little ability to guide a congregation.

Maybe your pastor or associate pastor left after only a very short time, and some members are still confused and angry, feeling betrayed. Some members may be angry with other members because they believe the pastor was treated poorly and left because of that poor treatment. Some of these may then decide to leave and go elsewhere.

You may have members who simply take a pastoral vacancy as the excuse to leave. When a pastor leaves, the departure creates not only dislocation but also a time of transition. Some church members are more committed to a pastor than to the congregation. When a pastor they like leaves a congregation, they also leave and go "pastor shopping."

Perhaps your session has already called in a "ghost-buster," an interim pastor. A good interim pastor can help a congregation identify its ghosts and bring them out in the open, where they can be recognized as "friendly" or "unfriendly." Your session has also taken the official steps to put together a search committee, and you have been elected. Be clear as a committee about how involved you want your interim to be with the search process. The presence of an interim pastor can significantly change a congregation's view of pastoral leadership.

Chapter 3

Getting Organized

Making the Presbyterian Way Your Own

Pastor or associate pastor nominating committees are under great pressure. Often they are the only group in a congregation with such an intense, time-consuming, and consequential task to accomplish on a time-limited basis. But remember: *Don't rush the process.* We live in an age of fast food, fast communication, fast-paced living in general. But it takes time to do a leadership search well, and you should be prepared to give your work all the time necessary.

This chapter will expand on the official guidelines for organizing your committee outlined in the manual that Call Referral Services sent you, so you may wish to review those guidelines now.

Organizing Your PNC/APNC

Yes, you have a very important task; but life goes on, your life. You now have an extra demand on your time, and that demand is an important responsibility. Despite this, you will not stop all those other activities and relationships that make up who you are: your work, your family, your friendships, your hobbies. There will still be grocery shopping to do and the lawn to be mowed or snow to be shoveled, maybe homework or college applications for a student who is a member of the team. There will continue to be everyday work for team members who teach, farm, practice law or medicine, install cabinets, or sell cars. In short, each member of your committee will continue to have other tasks.

Blend this new responsibility into your other work and play by setting priorities concerning what events and tasks you can afford to give time to. You may want to consider dropping some other church responsibilities for the duration of the committee's work. One search consultant commented that most pastoral searches last too long for most people to do "double duty" on both a search team and another major committee or group in the congregation without burning out.

The role of your leader is critical from the beginning, so let's address that subject as the first organizational matter.

You Have a Committee—Who Should Lead It?

You are looking for new leadership for your congregation, but first you need to settle your own committee leadership question. This matter ought to occupy the entire agenda at your first meeting. You will need a temporary moderator for your committee as you discuss the question of permanent leadership. I suggest that, if possible, you have as a temporary moderator someone who recently moderated a session committee or commission, someone who can guide you through the following considerations. Then you will either call for a vote or choose leadership by consensus of the committee.

Who is going to be your leader? How about having two

leaders? Comoderators or chairpersons are the choice of a number of committees because of people's busy and sometimes hectic schedules. If you go the direction of coleadership, make sure you choose this option for the right reasons. Some committees choose coleaders because two strong personalities vie for leadership, and rather than disappoint one they elect both. This is a bad reason. Two strong personalities with differing viewpoints about pastoral leadership can divide a committee and render it ineffective. Of course, one strong personality with a strong, unyielding viewpoint about pastoral leadership can also mislead a committee as a moderator or chairperson.

Be wary of choosing someone as your leader who is forthright about declaring she or he should lead because she or he knows exactly how the process should work and is sure about the type of person needed as the new associate pastor or pastor. Whoever is going to lead your committee should have strength of character, but the fundamental qualification is that the leader has the trust of the committee. Think in terms of choosing someone in whom everyone has trust and confidence. Your leader should have broad familiarity with your congregation and its ministry, someone who not only will be trusted within the committee but who has the trust and respect of the congregation.

You will need someone with good management insight and skills, especially if you have a large committee of more than eleven members. You need someone who can prepare meeting agendas that will keep you on track. The best committee leader is someone who can lead meetings effectively, can delegate tasks well, and can handle the tensions and anxieties that are inevitable in a group working under pressure. You want a leader or leaders who will give team members autonomy, help them to set goals, and free them to find their own way to reach those goals. This style is quite different from leadership that sets the goals and tells the committee how to achieve them. You want leadership that expects a lot of creativity from committee members and offers them considerable dignity. You want leadership that can coach the best from each team member. Think of your committee as a team that will be playing together, working together to accomplish a goal. The goal is not a competitive task of attempting to win a contest. The goal is to find the best possible leader for your congregation.

Team Building

With the question of leadership settled, plan your next meeting as a retreat. Take a day, or maybe a weekend including an overnight, for this retreat. Go to a different setting for this; do not meet at the church. Your leader or leaders can plan this event with two or three other team members. Or you could have an outside consultant guide you through some of the following matters.

The purpose of your time together, however you arrange it, is to get to know one another and to do team building. Don't assume that you do know each other. You will want to give some time to talking about yourselves, especially to telling your stories of faith. Have some fun. One committee took the Myers-Briggs personality test, and found that the results provided some humor and also helped members better understand one another's perspectives and comments later in their work. Have some discussion, some debate, and don't be afraid to have a few arguments. To have, early on in the process, good healthy debates on a variety of issues and viewpoints as you build trust will keep later debates from being interpreted as "personal."

Bunty Ketchum recommends that a committee spend

time discussing the skills each member brings to the search process. Often individuals have only limited awareness of the skills of other team members. By sharing them, some of the natural divisions of labor will become apparent.

Talk about the task ahead, and before the end of the session map out a plan. See Appendix B for an example of a plan to follow. It was put together by a search team seeking new leadership for a church of 2,500 members, but this model is adaptable and will fit any size church. Having a clear plan lends itself to reporting your work to the congregation with ease.

"Preparation is everything." I restore antique furniture as a hobby, and I learned early that it is a mistake to take shortcuts. Put the brakes on the "type A" personalities on your team who want to "start getting some candidate names." Names of candidates will come soon enough. You are going to be spending a considerable amount of time together, even if your search lasts only nine months. There is often an unspoken fear or apprehension on a search team, so talk openly with one another about who is afraid of what part of the task. "What if we call the wrong person?" Finding new pastoral leadership is a rigorous responsibility. One of the ghosts that may have surfaced in your congregation is a bad decision about a previous pastor. Talk honestly about the ghosts that members of your team have named. Discuss any other anxieties that have surfaced.

You should also have extensive conversation on the subject of making decisions. You are going to be making many decisions: when and where to meet, how long to meet, which PIFs to read, which candidates to visit, who goes to visit which candidate, what restaurants to eat in, and ultimately whom to nominate as the new pastor or associate pastor. How are you going to decide these matters? Will you decide by a consensus of the group or by a vote of the group, and if you choose to vote will you require a simple majority or a unanimous vote? Don't wait until you get to the point of nominating your candidate to decide how you're going to settle differences.

Most of us have experience with two models for group decision making: voting and developing a consensus of the group. A few members of your team may be familiar with Danny Morris and Charles Olsen's book *Discerning God's Will Together,* mentioned in chapter 1. Morris and Olsen offer spiritual discernment as a third alternative for decision making concerning church matters like the work of calling pastoral leadership. I urge you to examine and consider implementing their ten-step discernment process. This discipline goes against the grain of our fast-paced culture. I would be the first to argue that for matters like choosing a restaurant, voting is fine; but for most of your tasks I encourage you to work by consensus. Basic consensus means that everyone in the group is in agreement or comfortable enough with a decision to not stand in the way. Since your ultimate work is spiritual discernment, there will be times when consensus will take on the meaning of the Quaker perspective "the sense of the meeting." Morris and Olsen observe that in the Quaker tradition consensus expresses the sense of the meeting about how God is leading the community.

Finally, I also encourage you to talk about ground rules you wish to establish, such as starting on time, or that a team member should notify the moderator if she or he is going to be absent. Such matters as these and other ground rules should come from group discussion and not as directives from your leader. You are going to labor together for an extended period of time, and your efforts will cover a range of tasks in order to accomplish your final goal—calling new pastoral leadership.

Other Team Assistance

If you do not have comoderators, you will need to select a vice moderator to lead in the absence of your moderator. There will be a great deal of correspondence, and much of it may be by e-mail. The CRS guideline suggests that all correspondence be received and reviewed by the chairperson. Some committees follow that guideline; others elect a secretary. Talk over what would work best and be the most efficient procedure for your committee. You may also want to appoint a different person to take notes during meetings. A record of decisions and some account of the drift of discussion and conversation in your meetings will be important.

When Should You Meet?

Set your meeting schedule. This should be done on your retreat or when you have plenty of time to talk about a regular meeting time. Get agreement on what time slots will work reasonably well for everyone. Give yourselves some flexibility. The standard rule of thumb is once a week. But set a regular time on Monday, Thursday, Saturday, or whatever works. Set a time boundary; for example, 7:00–9:00 P.M., or 7:30–9:30 P.M.—no more than two hours. Some meetings may need only an hour of everyone's time. If you are not careful, you will exhaust yourselves with overextended meetings. I know of a committee that met every Saturday for three to five hours, however, and, after four months, began meeting during the week, since they felt they needed the extra time to exchange PIFs and information and to make phone interview calls. It was a committee with seven very committed members. Count on having impromptu meetings along the way. Sometimes a brief meeting right before or after the Sunday worship service will be most convenient.

Where Should You Meet?

The setting of your regular meeting is important. Meeting at one another's homes on a rotating basis seldom works well, and I advise against it, because someone is required to be host, time is often wasted on social niceties, and you often don't have the privacy you need. Pick a quiet place that's comfortable to work in, and where you will not be interrupted. Formal settings, such as an elaborately furnished church parlor, can lead to stiff, formal meetings. Think about and talk through what space would work best for your group. A big conference table and comfortable chairs will improve your effectiveness. Are there windows? Is there good air-conditioning and heating? This process may go on through summer and winter. Settle on the place and stick with it unless unusual circumstances make that impossible. A good setting will help keep your meeting efficient. One committee decided to meet in the law office of one of their members. Their reasoning was that by meeting away from the church and homes they were assured of confidentiality and privacy. The staff of the law office was accustomed to maintaining confidentiality, so unwanted disclosure of committee affairs was never a problem. Meeting in an office setting provided access to office equipment. This type of arrangement needs to be thought through and certainly wouldn't be available to all search teams.

Maintaining Body, Mind, and Spirit

The task of searching for leadership can be taxing, and decisions about where you meet, how often you meet, and how long you meet have an inescapable impact on the physical, mental, and spiritual well-being of the committee members. To my knowledge no one has polled members of PNCs and APNCs across the country and developed statistics on how many team members thought the experience deepened their faith and made them a better church member and how many never want to endure the experience again. The great majority of the people I have talked with experienced the former. Most agree that the work is demanding and sometimes tedious, but the rewards are deep friendships with team members and a profound appreciation for the breadth and depth of faith of team members and candidates.

Your regular meetings will be not only tedious but draining unless there is some "food for the soul." There will be homework, but you are going to learn a lot and give a lot, and at the end there will be a kind of graduation ceremony. You will sit in the congregation on the day of the installation of your new associate pastor or pastor with a sense of faithful accomplishment.

To assist you in maintaining body, mind, and spirit, I have listed a series of biblical stories and texts in Appendix C. There are also a few hymns. Like this entire book, the "soul food" I have listed is suggestive, not exhaustive. Begin your meetings with some led reflection on one of these texts or stories or some other biblical text or story, followed by prayer, led by one member or open for all team members. Close each meeting with prayer. But don't use prayer and scripture texts as bookends for your meeting. Let the Spirit move you throughout your meetings. Be honest with and open to God throughout your work. Offer God prayers of praise and thanksgiving *and* prayers of lament and frustration. If the prayers of lament and frustration are honest, then prospects are good that the prayers of praise and thanksgiving will be as well.

Reporting to the Congregation

Early in your work, perhaps after four or five meetings, develop a regular system for reporting the status of your work to your congregation. You may want to do this in a church newsletter or on a progress chart you post some-where in the church. Look again at the example in Appendix B. Your reporting does not have to be frequent (the PNC described in the appendix reported eight times over a fourteen-month time span), but regular reporting is helpful for a congregation to have a sense of your work. The less informed the congregation is, the more anxious it will become. The organizational chart you design for various tasks can be mailed out as a separate news item or included in your newsletter. If you have a Web page, post it there so candidates and other interested people can easily ascertain where you are in your process. Your reporting will not only help keep your congregation informed, but also build their trust in your work.

Confidentiality

Confidentiality is crucial to the effective work of your committee. I will address this subject later as it pertains to pastors' PIFs. But begin the practice now as you shape the way your committee goes about its work.

Chapter 4

Remembering Your Story

Telling Your Congregation's Story

Every congregation, large or small, young or old, urban or rural, has a story to tell. Most of the time, a congregation's story remains at the unspoken level. Everybody who is a part of the congregation just *knows*, without having to talk about it, that this church had a fire in 1965 or moved to a new location in 1976 or had a much beloved pastor in the 1980s or had a controversy in 1993 that led to some families leaving the church or started a soup kitchen ministry in 1996. These unspoken memories can have a powerful shaping effect on a congregation's life. When people say, "Now we're the kind of congregation that . . . ," they are working out of this unspoken story of a congregation's life.

There are times when it can be helpful to speak the unspoken, to call to active remembering the tacit narrative that forms a congregation's identity. Early in a search process is often such a time. One easy and enjoyable way to do this is to create a "time line" of your congregation's history. You can use a chalkboard or you can stretch a piece of butcher paper along the wall of your meeting room. Draw a long line and put the founding date of your congregation at one end and today's date on the other. Allow members of the committee to enter dates and events along the time line (you may want to do a little homework or ask someone in the congregation who knows the church's history to join you for this exercise).

The events I am talking about for the time line are those "happenings" in the life of the church that are talked about and remembered by the congregation. List whatever comes to mind: the names of pastors, new buildings, changes in worship, financial crises, and special celebrations. Have there been any strong experiences with pastoral leadership, positive or negative? What was the outcome? There will be joyful events and there may also be some events that the congregation does not like to talk about, but as you reflect on your history these events come to mind. Be honest in your reflections and your evaluation. When you have constructed your time line, spend some time pondering these questions: What kind of congregation have we been in the past? What kind of congregation would we like to be in the future? What will it take to work together toward that kind of future?

Once that review has been completed, look closely at your most recent pastoral history. Your former pastor or associate pastor is gone. Presbyterian pastors do come and go. What were the departure issues for your pastor or associate pastor? Some pastors go when you don't want them to, and some won't go when you want them to. Some pastors go after two years and some after twenty years. Some retire, some move to a new profession. Sadly, some pastors die suddenly. Some pastors are asked to go, and some are "forced" to go. The departure dynamics for pastors are different for large and small churches. Some congregations have large pastoral staffs, and associate pastors come and go all the time.

Some of the departure issues in your congregation may still bubble up from time to time, not only in the congregation but also in your committee. It is a mistake to ignore those feelings and responses and to rush on to find new leadership as soon as possible just to "fill the pulpit." *Don't rush the process.* Invite a consultant to meet with you, especially if you have some leftover issues that did not get settled by the congregation before you were elected, and those matters keep bubbling up.

Consider a Congregational Survey

Before moving too far along, you will perhaps want to take your congregation's pulse regarding their feelings about pastoral leadership, if that was not done before you were elected. You may already have your marching orders. A survey may have been included as part of the work of the mission study committee. If a survey has been completed, skip to the next step—writing your CIF. If not, here are two suggestions for gathering some information that can be used to guide your discernment work.

One way to gauge a congregation's views about pastoral leadership is to prepare a brief congregational survey to be handed out in church or mailed to every member. Be sure to put a deadline for returning it to the office, usually no more than two weeks after the survey is received. You will not get 100 percent participation, so don't wait for it. Remember that what you are looking for are impressions. Your survey ought to have four or five questions at most, and it should allow members to write comments in addition to answering the specific questions. See the sample survey in Appendix D.

Invite people to comment on their experiences of the church's life, what they would never want to change, and what they would like changed as soon as possible. You want to get a sense of what makes the congregation tick. Is it like a sailboat sitting in a lake with no wind? Where does your congregation expect the wind to come from? Or is your congregation on the move, with a desire to keep it going?

A second way of taking the congregation's pulse is through a series of informal gatherings of ten to twelve people. You can use the same kind of questions you would use in a survey. Members of the session and other elders and deacons can serve as moderators of these gatherings. Make sure you have a good scribe to take notes. The idea is to spend an hour or so over dessert in members' homes talking about the congregation and your leadership needs.

Once you have taken the pulse of the congregation, pull all your findings together into a summary statement. The commentary you collect will be of immense help for later work. If this initial assessment work is done well, it can guide the vision for new pastoral leadership.

Your next steps will depend on how your COM desires to proceed. Do you need to create a mission study? Many, if not most, presbyteries require that a mission study be done prior to the election of a PNC/APNC, so that may well have been done already. Your presbytery liaison can give you some guidance on this matter. Remember that presbyteries differ in what they recommend and require.

The purpose of a mission study is to reflect on some questions about the makeup of the congregation and the community. You may already have that information available. Some COMs will suggest that if you have research information that was used for another project in the church, you can use it. If you did that congregational survey, review that information. A good mission study will be a great help with the next big step: writing your Church Information Form (CIF).

The CIF Form

This form was revised and shortened in the fall of 1999 by the Office of Call Referral Services. Through its Church Leadership Connection, Call Referral Services created an internet Web site for matching services for churches and church professionals. The Web address for Churchwide Personnel Services and Leadership Connection is: www.cps.pcusa.org. There are instructions at that Web site for downloading the CIF. Download the form into a word-processing format. You can add your own personal touches to the form for referral on your own. After you have completed work on your CIF, a member of your committee with good computer skills can enter your information into the "live" database of forms. I will address how CRS circulates CIFs in the next chapter.

Writing Your CIF

Once again "preparation is everything," and you will want to construct the Church Information Form very carefully. The guidance in this section applies to all search committees, regardless of whether you are seeking a pastor or an associate pastor (there are some added issues about CIFs when you are searching for an associate, and I will explore those in the next section).

A good CIF should be the result of "blood, sweat, and tears." I tell my seminary students they should consider their PIF preparation to be equal to that of a term paper. Think of your CIF as a major report on your church that you will be publishing. A CIF is often the first impression that pastoral candidates have of your congregation. All pastoral candidates read CIFs carefully, looking for clues to a congregation's sense of identity and mission. A well-written and *easy-to-read* CIF will greatly assist the initial work of interpreting your congregation to pastoral candidates.

How do you create an easy-to-read document? Use the basic form of the CIF as your guide for the information needed, but also use your imagination and creativity as you put that information on paper or on your Web site. In these days of a shortage of Presbyterian clergy, you should present your congregation and its ministry in ways that invite effective candidates to consider your challenge. A PNC I know of produced a fine CIF that was read by a pastor who then commented to his wife, "That's me. I think I will end up going there." And he did.

Above all else, be honest in all the information you include in your CIF. Don't add "fluff and puff" material. Consider finding a CIF of a congregation in your presbytery that felt it had written an effective document. A number of churches are putting their CIFs on their Web pages, so do some searches for good church Web sites.

A well-prepared and well-written CIF will give the reader both a picture of and a feeling for your congregation. Now is the time to put into words the type of leadership needed by your congregation. What would that leadership look and feel like as your congregation experiences it? The document you put together should reveal what kind of leader you are seeking and be specific and clear about the kind of pastoral skills you seek. Don't overdescribe or overwrite. You can't be all things to all people. You are who you are as a congregation. You have a history, a faith story, to tell. What ought to come to the surface as you construct your CIF is a narrative of your congregation. Your CIF should contain the "talking points" you'll refer to when you reach the stage of interviewing candidates. *Don't rush this writing process.*

When you have all the parts of your CIF finished, have one person serve as your overall editor. Give this person the freedom to make sure the document reads well. Then the CIF should be given to a person with good computer skills so it can be sent electronically to a variety of recipients.

Since creating a good CIF is a multifaceted task, divide the preparation responsibilities. Your number will dictate how you divide the tasks. Revisit the variety of skills you have on your search team. A couple of team members who are good with statistics can gather the mission study census information about the community. A couple of others can put together the congregational statistics, while others work on the vision and mission portion. Two other team members can shape the language of the job description, that is, the kind of person you want your pastor or associate pastor to be and what you want that person to do. Spend some time as a whole team talking about the content of the position description.

Put up some newsprint, and brainstorm for some descriptive words to use. "We need a pastor who is . . ." Fill in the blanks. What personality traits do you want? Here are some examples I have seen in CIFs: passionate, dynamic, approachable, open, humble. Think about the specific characteristics you want: "We need a pastor who will . . ." what? "Who will relate well to all age groups in our congregation, especially the youth"; "who will have a sense of humor"; "who will keep the Bible in one hand and a newspaper in the other."

These are general examples. Think about your unique situation right now and remember that more than likely you will not find someone who perfectly meets all your expectations.

As you prepare your CIF, be careful how you view experience. Don't use a certain number of years of experience as your main qualifier. Long experience is not necessarily a guarantee of ability and wisdom nor is youth a guarantee of energy and creativity. Think in terms of what kind of experience you want candidates to have had. Let's say you are seeking a new pastor and your congregation has slightly more than one thousand members on the rolls, but many of those members are not active and attend worship only sporadically. Do you want someone who has ten years of experience in revitalizing a small congregation, or do you want someone whose experience has been as an associate pastor for five years in a vital congregation of a thousand members? If you are a small congregation, would it be better to have a recent seminary graduate just beginning ministry or would it be better to have a pastor nearing the end of his or her ministry and looking for a smaller congregation? What kind of challenges does your congregation offer? What type of candidate would rise to meet those challenges? When you begin to read PIFs, you can evaluate experience more effectively than if you have set an arbitrary number of years of experience in your CIF.

A critical component of your CIF is the matter of financial compensation. For help, consult with your presbytery office about the compensation packages of churches similar to yours in the presbytery, and talk with the official boards of other churches in your community that are also similar. Your discussion about this issue will be subject to the broader consideration of how your congregation views, raises, and uses money. Loren Mead, founder of the Alban Institute and an Episcopal priest with many years of pastoral experience in congregations, says money has more spiritual significance in the lives of people than almost anything else.

Mead's book *Financial Meltdown in the Mainline?* is a strongly worded attack on the mainline church's inability to connect the spiritual significance of money to the everyday life of the church. Mead observes that clergy have, by and large, opted out of engagement with the issue of money. My research with alumni/ae of Princeton

Seminary regarding the search process has shown that money, especially clergy compensation, is an extremely difficult subject for clergy and laity to discuss. I agree with Mead that part of our difficulty comes from our inability to distinguish between a materialism that comes from the incarnation ("God so loved the world that he gave his only Son," John 3:16) and a different kind of materialism that says this world is all there is. If the material world is all there is, then Madison Avenue is right. Whoever gets the most toys does win!

The issue for clergy is not how to get rich as a servant of Christ. It is how to be a good steward. Only a few pastors are overly concerned with money. More often, without good counsel or study, pastors do not give enough thought to a fair and adequate compensation package for themselves and, if applicable, for their families. Compensation packages are just that, packages, composed of a variety of parts: salary, housing, travel, professional expenses, health coverage, and matters such as continuing education and vacation. Ultimately members of your committee will negotiate the salary, the housing allowance or housing arrangement, and other parts of your compensation package. The package may have been determined by your session prior to your election. If not, get counsel from your session or the finance committee of the session regarding the range of the salary and housing for your new pastor or associate. You may find it necessary to go back to your session or finance committee to talk with them again if you find that your package does not meet the needs of candidates you talk with.

Searching for an Associate Pastor

The search for an associate pastor needs the same investment of time and energy as the search for a pastor.

Associate pastors, like pastors, are called by a congregation, and the call requirements specified in the *Book of Order* apply equally to pastors and associate pastors. Note those requirements in Appendix A.

If you are serving on an Associate Pastor Nominating Committee (APNC), more than likely your committee is small, perhaps five to seven members. Even though there will not be as many members to shoulder the load, you need to be as thorough in your reflection and in your preparation of a CIF for an associate position as you would be for a pastor.

Take care not to create a position description for an associate that assumes that an associate pastor will plug all the gaps and do all the tasks that are currently not being done at the church. I have read some associate pastor position descriptions that were ignored by seminary seniors because the positions were unrealistic about responsibilities. Some CIFs reflected a job description for an associate that looked like everything the pastor did not want to do.

The great majority of associate pastor positions have some variation of youth and Christian education responsibilities. Give thoughtful reflection to how you define these positions. Ponder the words of Kenda Creasy Dean and Ron Foster, authors of *The Godbearing Life: The Art of Soul-Tending for Youth Ministry*:

> The fundamental assumption behind this book is that youth ministry is not only for youth. Youth ministry is more about ministry than about youth, for Jesus Christ calls young people—like all of us—into ministry and not into a youth program. Christians who work with young people know that authentic ministry is more than a defensive posture, despite the fact that we inherit more than a century of youth ministry traditions designed to save youth from the evils of culture and to

preserve "the church of tomorrow." Youth ministry is primary—not secondary—ministry, for youth are called to bear the gospel in their own right. Youth have their mission fields as well as we do, and they look to the church to show them how to be the person God has called them to be in, and in spite of, their own culture. (P. 17)

No matter how you define your associate's responsibilities, the key to an effective associate pastor is her or his working relationship with the pastor. I served as an assistant pastor with two different pastors; both were supportive and helpful colleagues, and I learned what every minister on a staff must learn: sharing a vision and a positive working relationship with the senior pastor is absolutely essential to productive ministry.

Acquiring the skills of working as part of an effective team ministry is a transitional issue, especially for recent seminary graduates. They are moving from a seminary setting where collaborative work is not required to the setting of a congregation where it is. Sad to say, there are pastors who don't work collaboratively, and a capable associate can be threatening to them.

Define clearly the position and its responsibilities with the help of your pastor. Discuss what the working relationship will be with associates. Involve your pastor in the preparation of the job description. Do not attempt to compensate for some of your pastor's weaknesses when developing the responsibilities for an associate pastor without first talking candidly with your pastor about those weaknesses. One congregation designed a position description for an associate pastor with a number of administrative responsibilities. They then called someone for the position and informed the pastor that the new associate would be taking on some of his work. This was new information for the pastor, and conflict developed. The pastor ultimately took another call.

Work out the "division of labor" issues that will involve your pastor and associate pastor(s) on paper in your CIF and then discuss them frankly and thoroughly in the interview process with candidates.

Chapter 5

Going Fishing

Net-Working for Candidates

*F*ishing today is not what it was in the days of Peter, Andrew, James, and John. Sonar equipment can now locate whole schools of fish and trace their movement. You will want to use some of the newly available technology in your search for pastoral leadership. It is a rare search team that isn't using the biggest "fishing net" ever created, the World Wide Web, and you may be relying on the instant communication tools of e-mail and fax to communicate with candidates and references. Remember, though, this new technology cannot replace your labor, thought, wisdom, and discernment. You will have the best results and fish for candidates most effectively the old-fashioned way: careful, hard, prayerful work.

Finding new pastors and associate pastors is still a matter of throwing the net over the side and trusting, a practice known as "net-working." Now that you have prepared a "résumé" of your congregation—your Church Information Form—your task is to spread the word far and wide about the kind of church you are and the personality traits, skills, and character qualifications you seek in your new pastor or associate pastor.

Advertising Possibilities

Remember to get the word to your friends at the Personnel Services' Call Referral Services at the Presbyterian Center in Louisville so they can post your CIF on their Web site. I described in the previous chapter the mechanics of downloading the CIF and the purpose of composing it in the most reader-friendly style possible. Now you need to have a member of your committee versed in data entry fill out the CIF form at the PC(USA) Web site (www.cps.pcusa.org). That person may need to edit some of your narrative to fit the number of characters allowed. *Presbyterians Today, Monday Morning,* and *Presbyterian Outlook* are all journals that accept paid ads from churches for clergy searches. You will receive Personal Information Forms (PIFs) of candidates through the "front door," directly from the Call Referral Services at the Churchwide Personnel Services Web site office, and from other official delivery systems such as your committee on ministry or executive presbyter. You will also receive PIFs through the "back door." These PIFs will come as referrals from other pastors in the presbytery who are recommending friends, or perhaps from the pastor of your brother's church, who learned from him that you were on a search committee.

You should invite suggestions of possible candidates from members of your congregation and other sources. Send a copy of your CIF to the candidates whose names are suggested to you. And you are by no means limited to sending your CIF. Send an annual report and other interpretative material on the church and your community.

There are other "fishing holes or pools" you should consider. Go fishing in the "schools"—seminaries and divinity schools—with a letter or an e-mail and a copy of your CIF and other church material. Ask the president,

the director of alumni/ae relations, and the person responsible for placement at these schools for names of alumni/ae
they would suggest as candidates. Review the placement
Web pages of these schools, especially if you are seeking
someone just graduating from seminary.

When asking for names from anyone or from any-
where, highlight the criteria you are seeking in your new
pastor or associate pastor. When people offer names of
possible candidates to you "through the back door," ask
them to support their recommendations with specific
examples of how they meet your criteria. Also ask them
about the qualities I listed in chapter 1 concerning what
makes a pastor effective. You want candidates whom
other people believe in, trust, and have found to be effective. You want to know some of the specific qualities and
characteristics that make these candidates effective.

The PNC of a congregation with a thousand members
worked hard at finding the "right" candidate, but was
unsuccessful after two years. The specific qualities and
characteristics listed in their CIF fit the portfolio of the
typical omnicompetent pastor. I asked a member of the
committee to press to the next level of qualities and characteristics, to close his eyes and imagine what "Reverend
Right Fit" would look like. He responded, "Someone
with a lot of energy. Someone who is dynamic and energetic, and whose enthusiasm for ministry is contagious."
They found her about three months later and nominated
her to their congregation, which in turn extended a unanimous call to her. She is very energetic and vital, and her
energy and vitality are contagious. She is also a fine
preacher and an excellent administrator. I tell this story to
illustrate that you should press beyond the omnicompe-
tency portfolio and name the specific qualities and characteristics you consider to be most crucial in your new
pastor or associate pastor.

As you search for candidates, look for quality rather than quantity. You are not looking for "bragging rights" in the presbytery for having considered the most PIFs or candidates. Your goal is not a lot of fish, but ultimately the right one or two. I say two because there are some fine clergy couples who bring together a remarkable combination of skills for pastoral ministry, and they are proving to be very effective in a number of settings. Another combination to consider for a church searching for a new pastor and an associate at the same time is a team that has already worked effectively together, either as co-pastors or as pastor and associate pastor. You will need to have power to conduct such a search from your congregation.

Who Is the Best Candidate?

Is it better to look for someone who is seeking to move or for someone who is satisfied where he or she is? Neither type of candidate is necessarily better. You would be wise to consider both. There was a time when eight out of ten pastors would entertain a conversation with a search committee, whether they were looking to relocate or not. That's not the case anymore. Many pastors have spouses who work, and it may not be so easy for them to relocate. Many pastors are not willing to spend the time and energy talking with search committees unless they know they are seeking relocation.

Some search committees take the approach that they want someone who is not seeking a move, someone who is perfectly happy and satisfied where he or she currently serves. The work of those committees becomes a recruiting task. Their job is to "sell" a candidate on their position. This search model has been used successfully by many committees: the committee settles on a candidate and literally recruits that candidate, in some cases with some extra enticements such as a sabbatical or extended vacation period. This model can usually be used only by a search team that has the financial resources to engage in such a search and/or offer such inducements. One inherent problem in the model is that a PNC or APNC may promise more than a congregation can, or is willing to, deliver. A few search teams using the model have delivered a mismatch to their congregation.

Someone actively circulating a PIF is most often seeking a new challenge for his or her ministry gifts and skills. Sometimes circumstances in a pastor's family lead to consideration of relocating: children beginning school or leaving home for college; a spouse who is no longer working or who would like to relocate. Of course, it's possible that a few candidates who are actively looking are "burned out" and need a sabbatical more than a move. I know of pastors who relocate often, moving every three to five years. If you notice frequent moves on the PIF of a candidate who seems a good match for your congregation, you should inquire about those moves from references and directly in an interview with the candidate.

The Personal Information Form

The PIF like the CIF has been revised and abbreviated. The form is filled out by candidates on the same Churchwide Personnel Services Web site used for the CIF. Candidates can also download the form and format it in a word-processing format to make it more personal and easier to read.

Getting Acquainted through Paper: Reading PIFs

I mentioned that the search process for pastoral leadership takes a lot of people, a lot of paper, a lot of prayer, and a lot of patience. Here is where the paper begins to build up. Fifty PIFs x 4 pages = 200 pages x 9 committee members = 1,800 pages. One committee reported that by the end of its search process the documents accumulated by the committee formed a stack 4 1/2 feet high. Maybe new communications technology will cut down on the amount of paper.

Each committee member will need a PIF folder. Handle PIFs in a confidential manner. I cannot overemphasize the importance of confidentiality once you begin consideration of PIFs. No one except team members should see them, and you should not discuss PIFs with anyone other than team members. The "grapevine" or "gossip network" is astonishing in the larger church, and a few comments made to friends in confidence may well spread all around the denomination. Keep in mind that rumors about a pastor being considered by a PNC or APNC can be very damaging to her or his current ministry.

Devise a system for how you will copy, distribute, and ultimately destroy the PIFs you review. You should also devise a system for your reading and review work. The committee should decide as a whole if all members are going to read each PIF, or if you will have reading teams and delegate to each team the power to reject a PIF. I favor all team members reading all PIFs. Not every person on your committee will read a PIF the same way. Allow room for differences in the way you interpret what a candidate has said in her or his material.

Here's a suggestion for some PIF reading practice. Get three PIFs that are fairly different in style and content. Each team member should read them in advance and make some notes. Then devote an entire meeting to discussion of your reactions, so that members develop a sense of one another's views and perspectives.

Reading Is Easy (Most of the Time): Assessing and Evaluating PIFs

Read PIFs with a generous spirit. Some pastors write PIFs hurriedly and, being hurried, may not write well. A poorly written PIF is not necessarily a sign of a poor candidate. If a candidate has come highly recommended, she or he may be someone you don't want discounted just because a PIF did not measure up to your standards. Apply some grace to your reading work. On the other hand, what you see or read in a poor PIF may be exactly what you will get, namely, a pastor who does everything hurriedly and not well. By all means watch out for the slick PIF. It looks like a "marketing piece." You will recognize it when you see it. Often there is a lot of underlining, bolding, and bullets, and not much substance. Good content is the most important ingredient to look for in a PIF. This same counsel holds true for someone's Web site. Appearance is secondary, and should be valued only to the extent that it helps you read and understand the content.

Pay attention to your instincts and your intuitions while reading PIFs. One evening I commented to my wife about a perplexing PIF I had read that day. She asked what was wrong with it, and I couldn't really say. It contained reasonably good writing, but something about it disturbed me. The following morning I was listening to the weather forecast—"breezy and windy, mostly cloudy, with some sunshine." I said, "That's it, that's the problem with that guy's PIF. It's breezy and windy and mostly cloudy with only a little sunshine." A committee who read this man's PIF and then called him as their new pastor would be calling someone who was quite a talker and a self-promoter, but much of what he said would not be clear. He would have some fine qualities, but only rarely exhibit and use them. (Though I did not know the man at the time, I later learned I had made an accurate assessment.)

Part of the work of assessing and evaluating PIFs is the art of "reading between the lines." Ask yourself, "Why these words?" What is behind her telling this story? Look for the person behind or underneath the words and stories. Look for the traits and characteristics listed in your CIF. A candidate's PIF should introduce you to a person with a distinctive personality who has been called by God, who can sincerely describe how God has been at work in his or her life, and who can clearly describe an understanding of and practice of pastoral ministry. A good PIF should be transparent. You should be able to visualize the person who has written it. Learn to recognize what's "fluff and puff" and totally extraneous to what makes an effective pastor.

Snowflakes heavily influence my theology. We are all different. You don't see the differences in people until you get up close. Everyone's life is an interesting story. The challenge is to write our story so that a reader connects with the person who has lived that life. That's art. Make sure you read each candidate's PIF closely so you can see the differences between candidates. Look for writing that is graceful and grace-filled, humble, honest, evocative, and economical. You should be able to say "yes" or "no" after reading it. A "no" doesn't mean the person behind the PIF is not a good candidate. It means the candidate doesn't fit your needs. If you find you are building another stack of PIFs labeled "might consider later," that usually means those PIFs assigned to that stack are not clearly or distinctively written.

Bunty Ketchum's comments on this issue of "fit" may be helpful to you in rejecting PIFs. She observes that screening out applicants for any sought-after position is an acutely uncomfortable task. You may feel guilty and have some self-doubt. Committee members sometimes say, "It just doesn't seem fair to give a numerical rating to a person, especially not to an ordained minister. I haven't read enough. I don't know enough. I haven't seen enough. I only spent thirty minutes reading that PIF." Your thirty-minute reading may seem inadequate. But if ten members have spent thirty minutes each in reviewing the written record of a candidate, that person has received five hours of study. Although you may be working from a common set of criteria, all ten of you see different aspects of the candidate in the written record. You need not fear that any important strength has been overlooked by so many people. Trust your judgment. Trust the judgment of the other team members. Trust the Spirit's guidance of your work and your decisions.

More Observations about PIFs

Many presbyteries require candidates to submit a PIF to the presbytery's COM or executive presbyter before a search team can seriously consider them. If you pursue candidates who do not have PIFs and who resist writing them, you may need to negotiate with your COM about the possibility of interviewing those candidates.

Assessing and evaluating the PIFs of candidates just graduating from seminary may need a different perspective. Seminary seniors are coming from an institution that measures work by grades. Seminaries value independent (sometimes even solitary) work habits and reward academic achievement. Congregations value leadership, maturity, stability, teamwork, and openness, and reward wisdom and practical knowledge. Seminary seniors sometimes write overly worded and somewhat academic PIFs. They go overboard writing about their school field education work because they are trying to make up for lack of experience. When evaluating a new seminary graduate, you should look beyond the seminary to other "life experiences"—summer jobs, volunteer work, even family and friends.

Protocol

Do we have to answer all these people? Yes! *How* you go about responding to self-referred PIFs and other communications from candidates is up to you, but I encourage you to develop a system for acknowledging that you have received candidates' PIFs. Don't put the burden of devising this plan and all other correspondence on your secretary. Work out the system together. A postcard will do just fine for the early acknowledgments. Make sure it goes to a home address. All your correspondences should go to the PIF "preferred" address. You will need letters later on. Look at the examples in Appendix E. Your acknowledgment is not only a considerate gesture; it is part of good communication.

When you are writing letters rejecting candidates, use the operating principle of "less is better." You should not go into great detail about your reasons. Insert a paragraph in a brief form letter or e-mail that says something like "We have studied your materials and are now in the difficult part of our search, which requires narrowing our pool of candidates. Although we were favorably impressed with your credentials and the fine ministry you are doing at your present church, we decided that the fit between your credentials and our needs was not close enough."

An extra word of caution about rejection letters. Be sure to keep straight which PIFs have come from the pastors themselves and which have come from other sources. Many ministers have had the slightly insulting experience of receiving a rejection letter out of the blue from a committee they had no idea was looking at them as a candidate. If a third party gave you a pastor's PIF and you decide this pastor is not a match for you, you may or may not wish to inform the third party—but you do not need to write a declining letter to this pastor directly; indeed, it is not appropriate to do so.

Evaluating Preaching Skills

If your committee has the financial resources, travel to see and hear candidates. Some evaluation sheets that may be useful on such visits are included in Appendixes G and H. Discuss whether you want to make these visits unannounced or to arrange an interview during your visit.

One way to sample a candidate's preaching is to request tapes of recent sermons. Remember, though, that as good as modern technology has made audio- and videotapes, there is nothing like experiencing a candidate's preaching in a live worship setting. Should you request audiotapes or videos? Strange as it may seem, I prefer audiotapes to videotapes. Audiotapes encourage a focus on content and meaning rather than appearance. Most videotapes made in worship are done on home equipment, and the result can be poor and even misleading. For example, a close-up shot of a preacher may cause expressions and gestures to appear exaggerated, when they are quite fitting in the large space of a sanctuary. Moreover, Hollywood and television have corrupted our sensibilities and influenced the way we view people. Be careful about getting caught in the prejudices of our cultural judgments about people. What pastors look like in a videotape of a worship service has little correlation to their effectiveness in ministry. Treat people the same way you treat paper. Appearance is secondary to content.

To cite a sad example of mistaking appearance for substance: A good friend of mine did an outstanding job in a field education position in a large, influential congregation while he was in seminary. He was informed by an elder in the congregation that he would make a fine pastor but would never be considered as pastor at her church because he was too short. All their pastors had been at least six feet tall!

Checking References

Ultimately what you most want to know about your candidates is if they can do the job and if they are willing to do the job. What may happen to them while they are in the job that would keep them from being able and willing is unknown and largely unpredictable.

I will comment more on gathering helpful information from references in the next chapter. My rule of thumb is to talk to references after you have had a preliminary interview with a candidate, asked some questions either by phone or in person, and/or had some direct, personal experience with the candidate, like a meal. You will ask better and more relevant questions of references if you first talk with the candidate and ask good, insightful interview questions.

Remember, candidates understandably pick references who will speak favorably about their abilities. You should go beyond the first tier of references to a second level, of individuals who know your candidates well and who may be suggested to you by the initial references.

Chapter 6

It's Time to Talk

Insights on Interviewing

I think interviewing is the most enjoyable part of the work of seeking new pastoral leadership, but it is also the most challenging. In the Preface I indicated that I still remember interview settings and conversations of more than twenty years ago. The memories are still with me because, while some interviews were very good and some were not very good, all were significant memories.

While serving at a seminary for the last thirteen years, I have seen mismatches happen in calling pastoral leadership that are directly attributable to poor interviewing, interviews that were rushed or unprepared for—sometimes by a search committee, sometimes by the candidate, and sometimes by both. The results have been congregations that did not get what they thought they were going to get in the new pastor or associate pastor, and pastors or associate pastors who formed mistaken expectations about their new congregations.

Especially in the church context, we ought to work to avoid such mismatches, if for no other reason than good financial stewardship. Calling and relocating a pastor costs money. But there are more important reasons for care, including the general well-being of congregations and pastors. Dissolved relationships because of mismatches leave wounds that can take a long time to heal.

You can make or break your search for new pastoral leadership by how you treat the interview process. Your committee's interviews of candidates will play a crucial part in the search process as a setting for testing pastoral credibility. Each member of your search team will develop opinions about a candidate's ability to be your pastor or associate pastor in the setting of an interview. In my judgment, the interview process can lead effectively to a productive match between your congregation and the candidate you ultimately call if core issues and ingredients related to the match are addressed and resolved satisfactorily by both you the search team and the candidate *prior* to the call's being issued or accepted. I will address what I believe are seven core interviewing issues later in this chapter.

As your committee moves on and begins to evaluate impressions of candidates, you will wish there were rules you could follow. Unfortunately, it is impossible to develop a list of infallible rules for all interviewing, or even specifically for interviewing pastoral candidates. A significant amount of material has been written on the subject of interviewing, but ultimately interviewing takes place between people, and we are far too individualized to be reduced to a formula.

Interviewing brings you in direct contact with candidates. Your work is no longer at a distance, or coolly objective. When you begin interviewing, your perspective on candidates will be subject to the impressions that a telephone call or a face-to-face meeting creates. With a phone call you will hear a voice, perhaps for the first time. You like the voice. You don't like the voice. You are neutral about the voice. Get ready to start evaluating your subjective impressions.

The Artful Methods of Interviewing

Interviewing is an art. It is subject to our impressions and opinions. All of us participate in some form of interviewing every day. It is the way we gather and give information. When you think about what takes place in your daily conversations, you discover that there are a vast number of variables in your information exchanges. We begin to develop our artistic skills in interviewing at a young age. "What is that?" "When are we going to get there?" And the classic child's interview question, "Why?"

An art is a skill or power of performing certain actions, and that skill or power can be acquired by study, experience, or observation. Cooking is an art, and so is fly-fishing. Interviewing, cooking, and fly-fishing are also sciences. There are methods to interviewing, cooking, and fly-fishing that can be learned.

People who have studied the subject of interviewing have long known that some people, because of the nature of their work and experience, acquire skill in interviewing, sometimes consciously, usually unconsciously. These people include lawyers, doctors, nurses, reporters, police, pastors, counselors, and personnel managers. For some of them interviewing becomes a science, some of whose basic principles they are able to formulate and organize into a method, a systematic body of knowledge.

Each member of your search team is an "interview artist." Each of you should try to expand on your interview experience and observation and consciously develop your skill by study and further experience and observation, so that you can formulate and organize some basic principles and develop your own "methodology" or "science" for interviewing.

Many of us have been influenced by the methodology or approaches to interviewing and hiring and employment practices of the secular world. Wilbert Scheer wrote the "Bible" of personnel employment—the *Personnel Administration Handbook*. He writes that most interviews are confused bluffing sessions: no one knows for sure who is trying to impress whom. For Scheer, the interview is the determining factor in the employment procedure. He notes that the purpose of an employment interview is to collect information, to combine and classify it, and to help predict the likelihood of the applicant's being able to perform the job successfully. While the applicant is on his or her best behavior—dressed in his or her best, polite, and cooperative—the interviewer must work extra hard to create an environment of trust and even relaxation so as to get a picture of the applicant's true self, of how he or she will function later, on the job. Remember, you are not just "hiring" someone. You are seeking a candidate to nominate to your congregation so they can "call" that person. Your work is a task of spiritual discernment.

Interviewing as Courtship

Over the last thirteen years I have studied the matchmaking work of churches looking for pastoral leadership and candidates looking for the right place. I have discovered that, given all its theological underpinnings, this venture actually has many similarities to the process of courtship and marriage. At first, committees and candidates engage in cautious "first meetings" through phone conversations, letters, e-mails, and the exchange of PIFs and CIFs. Once the "spark is struck," real courtship begins. The final stages of the romancing narrow down the number of dating relationships, and finally a marriage proposal is offered. One of the keys to satisfaction and effectiveness in pastoral ministry has to do with the ability of both search committees and candidates to ask each other the right questions, so that neither party has a lot of surprises once the marriage is made.

Two pitfalls in both courtship and interviewing are attempting to balance the subjective and objective dimensions of discovery and recognizing the difference between superficial and substantial information. Candidates and search teams, like potential marriage partners, sometimes base their love for each other on appearances or on emotional effect. I have heard expressions such as "He has the looks and voice of a preacher" from members of a PNC sometimes, giving the still prevailing image of the minister as male. (The church hasn't quite decided what it wants to do with "her" looks and "her" voice.)

I know of committees that spent a year or more studying the needs of their congregation and preparing profiles for the kind of pastor who would meet those needs, and then in one interview were dazzled by a candidate who was "all glitter and no substance" and did not match the profile at all. Usually in such cases one party or the other files for divorce in less than two years.

A word of caution: Some pastors substitute a stage persona for a more fundamental and authentic identity. That stage persona is what they think a pastor ought to be, a role to be played. Whether you are seeking a pastor or an associate pastor, you want someone who is secure in his or her sense of self, someone who can clearly define herself or himself. Some pastors are outstanding interviewers but seriously flawed as pastors. On the other hand, some candidates don't interview well but are outstanding pastors. Build your interviewing around questions that will help you discover candidates' talents and skills and their flaws and weaknesses. Review Appendix F for basic types of interview questions.

What about the person who interviews well but turns out to be a poor pastoral match? Perhaps the "outstanding interviewer but flawed pastor" has, subconciously or conciously, been using an approach to interviewing described by Robert Half, a business management consultant who has written extensively on job searches, especially in his book, *The Robert Half Way to Get Hired in Today's Job Market.* Half argues that, most of the time, finding a good job has very little to do with one's qualifications and personal attributes and everything to do with interviewing technique. There is a big difference, claims Half, between having the "right" qualifications and getting hired on the basis of them. The brutal truth about job hunting, Half argues, is that the most qualified person is not necessarily the person who gets the job. Rather, it is the most persuasive person, the person best able to convince the people doing the hiring that he or she is the right person for the job. Half believes the art of finding a good job, in other words, consists not so much in *having* what you need, but in *using* what you have to the best advantage. Thus a pastor who is a "persuasive talker" but has few of the essential skills to be a good pastor will *use* "talking" to the best advantage.

Truly effective pastors are not just "looking for a good job," however. They are seeking a call. Make sure your candidates *have* the gifts and skills that your congregation *needs.* You can better judge candidates' gifts and skills by understanding some of the "science" of interviewing. An interview has a variety of parts, much as a sentence has nouns, adjectives, verbs. My high school English teacher taught the science of sentence structure by using a diagram of the different parts. My compound sentences with participial phrases and infinitives scattered here and there looked like a strange little picture, but the picture made sense.

I am not suggesting that you "diagram" your interview experiences, but I do urge you to pay attention to all of the parts of your interviews such as "body language," "nonverbal interactions," "situational variables," and "negative and positive perceptions." Once you begin interviewing candidates, these different parts of the interviewing process will become as familiar to you as verbs, nouns, and direct objects.

Initial impressions and perceptions of candidates will be part of each of your interviews. There are "situational variables"—unexpected events or circumstances that will occasionally influence effective interviewing. One seminary senior told me that, during his interview with a committee, an air conditioner compressor outside the window was making so much noise that neither the search team nor the candidate could hear clearly. The noise was disturbing to the interview process, and annoyed both parties, but no one did anything about it. Another senior went off campus for a second interview with a committee, and on arriving was told that one of the search team members had been seriously injured in an auto accident the day before. The committee went on with the interview, but their minds and hearts were not in it. A host of "situational variables" can have an impact on your interviews, so be alert for them.

You should also pay attention to another part of each interview, the wide variety of "body language," or nonverbal interactions, we all use in conversation: head nods, facial expressions of all kinds, speaking pauses, hand gestures, arm and leg movements, posture in general, touches, yawns, glances at a watch, glances out a window, eye contact or lack of contact. All of these are forms of communication. Learn to evaluate the "body language" of your candidates.

Interview Ingredients and Issues

After informal surveys of seminary graduates and some other research, I have identified what I believe are essential elements or categories the interview process should address:

1. Self-Awareness
2. Authenticity
3. Theology
4. History
5. Leadership Style/Work Schedule
6. Money
7. Nature of the Community

You should have specific questions you prepare to ask each candidate. And you should prepare to be asked specific questions by each of your candidates (see examples in Appendix I). But I urge you to approach your interviews with the idea of establishing a conversation with your candidates.

1. *Self-Awareness*—A good beginning question to ask is the classic: "Tell us a little about yourself." No matter how a candidate answers that question, you will have information to assess. Glimpses of self-awareness, authenticity, leadership style, and perhaps other ingredients will be offered for evaluation. You may get more information than you wanted, but an excessive answer to any question is data to be appraised. Long answers to this question may mean there is more self-deception than self-awareness in a candidate.

Keep in the back of your mind the qualities Edward White in the article we cited in chapter 1 suggests are needed for a pastor to empower laity. Is this pastor secure in his or her sense of self? Can this pastor clearly define her- or himself? How grounded would this pastor be in the midst of ambiguity and conflict? How clear is this pastor about his or her own possibilities and limitations?

2. *Authenticity*—Authentic means "real." Is the candidate the genuine article, or someone who is merely role-

playing at being a minister. The subject of authenticity has to do with pastoral credibility and underlies all the other ingredients in the interview process. It is the yeast that makes the dough rise, and it contains two additional components: integrity and honesty. It is my firm conviction that if these ingredients are not in the search process, the final match or call will fall flat. Candidates will ask questions to test your authenticity: Are these people simply "playing church" or are they seeking to be faithful disciples of Jesus Christ?

Integrity has to do with a set of values that are sound and transparent and remain consistent throughout the process, beginning with PIFs and CIFs. Honesty has to do with candor and forthright give-and-take that are necessary in interviewing. Your questions should probe and test the ability of each of your candidates to be a credible interpreter of the gospel. Ask your candidates to describe a time of crisis in their ministry, a time when they had to wrestle with the mystery of God.

3. *Theology*—The issue here is whether there is sufficient overlap in the theological perspective and convictions of the candidate and the congregation, thus allowing for the development of trust and pastoral credibility. Questions and conversations around this issue should identify and clarify critical theological terminology for both you and the candidates. Don't spend time and energy worrying about labels such as conservative, moderate, liberal, evangelical. Questions about how candidates lead Bible study and approach Christian education will draw out theological convictions. Ask candidates to describe their ministry in a particular family crisis in their congregation, a death, a marriage, or a baptism. You should engage your candidates in conversation about their ministry in general, and their theology will become evident.

4. *History*—Start your look at a candidate's history with positive questions: "Tell us about a few of your successes." Follow that question with, "What do you think made you effective in that area?"

A look at your candidate's past is important for what it may indicate about the future. Past problems need not indicate future ones, but should be explored and assessed. A pastor I know of has been asked to leave three different churches. Did the second church find out what happened in the first church? By the third church, one wonders if serious reference checking had been done. I will discuss reference checking later, but remember, most first-line references do not want to talk with members of a search team about a candidate's flaws or weaknesses in such a way as to keep the candidate from being seriously considered. Everybody participates in a kind of "verbal dance," trying to make the candidate appear as attractive as possible.

I have participated in those "verbal dances" when commenting on a few seniors. A good reference should make the candidate attractive, and if necessary talk about what might be viewed as a negative. I once served as a reference for a good friend who is a recovering alcoholic. A committee chair asked me, "Is there anything else about this candidate that you think we should know?" This question told me that the committee had the candidate on their short list and was checking to see if the candidate had any "skeletons in his closet." I responded to the question by saying my friend was a recovering alcoholic. I then told my questioner that I brought that fact to his attention, not because I thought it was a problem or weakness, "a skeleton in the closet," but because I thought it was a great strength and that my friend drew on his recovery as a pastoral aid in counseling members of his congregation. I thought my friend's history with alcoholism had been turned into a positive dimension of his ministry.

5. *Leadership Style/Work Schedule*—There should be some ranking of the various pastoral activities that would indicate how a candidate and your search team view the priorities of pastoral responsibilities. Get the work expectations of your congregation out on the table. Talk about what a work week/month/year might look like. Your interview process should aim at eliminating as many surprises as possible. Don't end up after the fact saying, "He lied to us. He told us he would spend quality time with the youth program." Find out what "quality" time is, and reach agreement on it. Get agreement on who sets the work schedule and who monitors it, especially if you are interviewing a candidate for an associate pastor position.

6. *Money*—I commented earlier, while discussing a compensation package to include in your CIF, that the subject of money has broad and far-ranging implications. The issue does include how your congregation views, raises, and uses money, and it includes the compensation not just of the pastor but of all your employees. Budgets should be a topic for your interview conversation as you talk with candidates about financial stewardship, theirs and yours. If you have concerns about a decline in your congregation's financial stewardship, you should discuss those concerns with candidates. Talk about bequests, planned giving, and endowments with your candidates.

Compensation packages are not a recent invention of the church; if you read the terms of calls of pastors two hundred years ago, congregations provided a place to live, two sides of beef, one pig, a barrel of flour, and an agreement for time off—and, yes, even a keg of whiskey. (Presbyterians in colonial America received kegs of whiskey "for medicinal purposes.") Times have changed, and so have the components of the packages. Look at the list of components in Appendix A about terms of the call.

Candidates will ask questions that seek to find out if

you will support their ministry through not only time for continuing education, but also adequate compensation for it.

7. *Nature of the Community*—This category includes two types of information that will be important for candidates to know about your church: sociological information pertaining to the geographical area surrounding your church and information about the congregation itself as a community. You can answer candidates' questions most effectively by reviewing your congregational story—if you developed a "time line" early in your process, you may wish to review it with the candidate. This information is what candidates are most anxious to learn about, so be prepared to discuss their questions about your history and what makes you "tick" as a congregation. Equally important will be the job of determining if candidates are suited for your community.

I offer these seven matters as suggested topics for interview conversations. You will have other issues that you will want to address as well.

Practice Makes Perfect

Well, maybe nothing achieves perfection, but practice at any task will help you improve your ability and skill. A little practice interviewing will help your committee define and refine its abilities and techniques and help members improve one another's questions. Review the material on interview questions in Appendix F and develop a set of questions that you plan to ask each candidate. Have a few team members role-play, for practice, the candidates represented by the PIFs you read, or have a pastor in a nearby church role-play a potential candidate and critique your interviewing technique and questions. You want to be at your best when you begin your real interviews.

I can tell you from experience that candidates want to be at their best too. If there is even a slight resemblance between the search process and courtship, there is bound to be some anxiety for you as committee members and for the candidates. Interviewing is a mildly threatening experience. More than likely the pulse rate goes up for everyone. A candidate can feel a bit intimidated. Good interviewing should be neither a bluffing session nor an interrogation.

When Does Interviewing Begin?

Thus far you have been exchanging a considerable amount of information, but it has all been on paper, by e-mail, or via a Web site. Interviewing begins when there is live conversation, when you start talking directly with candidates. In most cases, your initial interviews will be phone calls or live video conferencing. There are some matters you should consider prior to making phone calls to prospective candidates. Who makes the call? When? What will the content be? How long do you want the call to be? Will it be a conference call with more than one participant? Don't approach phone calls with candidates haphazardly. First impressions do matter.

Let's say you decide to make some conference calls. Be sure to arrange the calls in advance. Be pleasant, and respect the candidate's time. Begin with something like: "Hello, Louise, this is Dean Foose, a member of [identify your committee, church, and community]. Is this a convenient time to talk briefly? Thank you. Our search committee would like to have a conference call with you. We meet regularly on Thursday evenings and would like to schedule a thirty-minute conversation with you. Would seven to seven thirty next Thursday evening be suitable for you?"

Conference calls can be longer or shorter, but make sure you establish what the length will be. Treat such calls like a face-to-face interview. Introduce the entire committee by name. A conference call is not the best setting to get to know someone, but you can gain some good impressions and some valuable information. By the time this book is published, communication technology may be such that all telephone calls will be face-to-face.

Certainly the face-to-face interview provides the best setting. You can perceive feelings and emotions revealed in body language. You may ask a question and receive not only a verbal answer but also a frown or a smile or even a laugh. You may ask a question and see apprehension or anxiety on the face of the candidate. Now you have to think about what that apprehension might mean.

Arranging Interview Visits

If you want to interview a pastor who is currently serving a congregation, plan to go visit him or her on a Sunday when he or she is preaching and arrange in advance an appropriate time and setting to discuss your congregation and his or her candidacy. Debate the advantages and disadvantages of dividing your committee for these visits. If you are traveling all over the country for visits, by all means divide your committee. If the visit can be accomplished in one day, including driving round trip, the entire committee should go. Bunty Ketchum offers this perspective: She writes that two or three committee members interviewing a candidate is a far easier technique than having the whole group conduct the interview; however, they then have the burden of passing on their findings to the rest of the committee, and in the transfer some information is lost.

Maintain your confidentiality and the confidentiality

of the pastor you are visiting. Don't all sit in the same pew, don't go to adult education classes, do attend all services, don't take notes during services, save the bulletin and other paper such as newsletters and brochures, and be discreet about meeting your candidate in a restaurant.

Develop a mutually agreed on schedule with the candidate, and give her or him flexibility in arranging the schedule. An interview over lunch immediately following a busy Sunday morning will not be the choice of every pastor. Ketchum believes that any interview lasting more than two hours is an imposition on any person. She emphasizes the importance of planning specific questions. Who will ask what question? Think about what questions you have for each specific candidate. What aspects of his or her ministry have given you puzzling or contradictory messages?

After any interview, phone or face-to-face, all team members should immediately write down impressions, noting as much as they can about traits, qualities, and characteristics of the candidates. Prepare a check sheet for such use. Have a place for expanding on the checklist. If you are seeking someone who is passionate about mission and outreach or evangelism, be specific about what indicated a candidate's passion, for example.

Preparing for Candidates' Questions

Plan your interviews so candidates will have an appropriate amount of time to ask questions. The time does not have to be exactly equal since some of their questions may be answered as you ask your questions. Some of their questions will come from the information in your CIF. They will ask you both to expand on that material and to interpret some of it. Review the seven ingredients I discussed earlier. All those issues are applicable to you as you represent your congregation to candidates. They will have questions about your history, about your role expectations for them, and about your congregation's theological perspective and worldview. They will probe to find out about the self-awareness of your congregation. I have included in Appendix I types of questions candidates might ask. Be a bit concerned and suspicious if a candidate does not ask you any questions. He or she may be too anxious to please.

Written Questions for Candidates

If you can't deduce the answers to your written questions from your candidate's PIF, then ask the questions in a phone call. If you are seeking information about a specific subject or issue, ask for copies of sermons about those subjects or issues. Or ask for writing samples from church newsletters.

Interviewing for Associate Pastor Positions

Most committees searching for associate pastor leadership will have a smaller pool of candidates than those seeking pastors. Once again, the key to effective work on the part of associate pastors is their working relationship with the pastor. A poor relationship with a pastor in a current situation should not automatically rule out a candidate's consideration by your committee. Mismatches between pastors and associates often have little if anything to do with the pastoral abilities of either. The mismatches are often related to a difference in leadership style or personality, and some conflicts between pastors and associates are gender-related. Include your pastor in the consideration of candidates early in your search process. If you are planning a visit to a seminary to interview, by all means include your pastor in that visit.

It goes without saying—but I will say it anyway—that your pastor should have final veto over candidates for associate positions. I have had seniors "fall in love" with a search committee and congregation but express strong reservations about working with the pastor, and then go ahead and accept the call with parting words to me: "There may be some rough sledding at first, but I think I can get him to see things my way." Guess who is asked to look for a new call within the year?

Narrowing the Pool of Candidates

You will work at reducing the number of candidates under consideration throughout the search process. You begin that work early, as you read and reject PIFs. Once you begin to interview, you will again narrow the number of candidates you want to seriously consider. You will be working from some ratings scales you developed around the specific criteria you are seeking in a new pastor or associate pastor. Continue your courtesy contacts with all your candidates, letting them know where you are in your process. Ask them to let you know if they no longer want to be under consideration.

At some point you should develop a "short list" of two, three, or four final candidates. These are the strong candidates you want to meet with at length and introduce to your setting, so they can see the church and the community and have some in-depth conversation with the search committee. You may want to keep another list of eight to ten second-tier candidates in case none of the candidates on your short list is chosen.

Interviewing Your Short List

When you have developed your short list of final candidates, put together a consistent way of hosting them, so that each candidate is seen in the same set of circumstances. Each candidate should experience the same plan; for example: dinner Friday night with the entire committee, a tour of the building Saturday morning with three members, lunch with three other members, and a tour of the community with three others. Use each of these settings for specific questions. Don't exhaust your candidates with a whirlwind tour of everything. Plan some rest time on the schedule.

I vividly remember a two-day whirlwind interview that began after a three-hour plane trip, on a Sunday after preaching in the church I served. Two members of the committee met my wife and me at the airport at about 6 P.M. We received a thorough "grilling" on the way to the church, where we had dinner with seven members of the eleven-member committee. After an hour and a half of eating and answering questions, we got to our hotel room about 10 P.M. Monday was spent on a tour of the city and the church, with no free time. My wife was taken to the airport for a flight home at 5 P.M., and I had dinner out with part of the search team, some of whom I had met and some whom I had not. The evening ended about 9:30 P.M. Tuesday consisted of meeting with various staff people, including lunch with one. At 4 P.M., I met the entire committee for the first time for an hour's "wrap-up" in the large formal church parlor. I sat in an overstuffed sofa and could easily have dozed off. The first question was "Tell us a little about yourself." After eight to ten minutes of rambling, I noticed a team member looking out the window of the church parlor and tapping a pencil on his notepad. It dawned on me that I had lost those folks in my review of growing up in Texas and recounting my college and seminary years and my various pastorates. At 5 P.M. the group thanked me for my time, and after learning there was not going to be any dinner opportunity I rummaged a cheese sandwich from the church kitchen with the help of a committee member before I caught my 7 P.M. flight home.

I had no advance notice of what that interview schedule was going to be. Nor was I given a schedule when I arrived. I learned from the experience that not all search committees plan a specific schedule. I encourage you not only to plan one, but to give it to your candidates in advance.

Discussion of Compensation

At some point during the visit of each of your final candidates, an informal discussion of your terms of call should be included. You are not negotiating the final terms at this point, but rather discussing the practical needs of the candidates and your compensation package. This discussion should be with no more than three members of your search team. It could take place during the tour of the community or the church property. Use the compensation page of your CIF as a guide for your conversation. A discussion of money, particularly a compensation package and all its components, needs integrity and honesty. Discussing such items as health insurance, social security, and an adequate utility allowance is good practical theology. Inform candidates whether malpractice insurance is a part of the umbrella liability policy for the church.

Information about salary and compensation is spelled out more in CIFs than in PIFs. What you most need to know from each candidate is whether your total package is close to meeting the candidate's needs and desires.

Following each of your interviews with candidates on your short list is the time to do detailed reference checking.

How to Talk with References

Robert Dingman devotes an entire chapter in his book *In Search of a Leader* to "The Fine Art of Reference Checking." He points out that a major flaw in the selection process with most Christian groups is that they are usually satisfied too easily by what the search committee sees on paper and learns from interviews. He offers some good reasons for this. Christians are particularly prone to believing the best about people, particularly about spiritual leaders. Both search teams and candidates put their best foot forward and tend to conceal their flaws and limitations. Good reference checking takes time, courage, and skill. Team members often have too much confidence in their ability to "read people" or to get divine messages about the candidates.

I believe the key to reference checking is how you frame the questions you ask. Ask questions that relate to how a reference knows the candidate. If you are asking about preaching style and content, make sure the reference has heard the candidate preach, preferably more than once. Your questions to references should follow up on specific concerns that grow out of your interviews with candidates. Does she share responsibility easily? Does he delegate responsibilities that should be his? Would the success and effectiveness of an associate threaten him? How does she respond to crisis situations? Ask references to describe specific critical incidents or issues, such as how the candidate reacted to budget crises and other critical incidents, or how he handled confidences. You want to know specifics about how these candidates performed as a pastor. You want pastoral leadership attuned to and aware of the world. Ask references about a candidate's community involvement and what she or he reads. If you are seeking someone with effective administrative skills, ask references to describe specific, effective use of administrative and management skills.

Written references often aren't worth the paper they are written on. Many people will not give substantive written references because of a pervasive spoken or unspoken fear of being sued. That fear may not be well founded statistically. However, it is a rare presbytery executive who will put his or her honest perspective on paper. They may talk "back door" with somebody at their level, such as another presbytery executive.

There are legal issues to take into consideration. Let's say you asked me to comment on a candidate you were considering, and I wrote back and gave you a reason why I would not extend a call to that person. Later, you told the candidate that the reason you were not extending a call was because of what I said in my letter, and you gave the candidate a copy of my letter. The letter could be used, with good cause or not, in a time-consuming and expensive lawsuit against me. Knowing this, I would be reluctant to put my thoughts into writing.

Once you have concluded interviewing your short list, you are nearing the point of nominating a candidate to your congregation. You are near the "big decision." You may want to revisit a reference or two with a few other questions or speak to some other people who know your final candidates. Make use of second-tier references. Ask the references your candidate gave you for a name of someone they think would be helpful to talk with. Your questions of references at this point should follow up any new information or intuitions gained from the visits with your short list of candidates. When speaking with people other than the references given you by candidates, tell them your conversation should be confidential.

Chapter 7

The Big Decision

*T*he Presbyterian way of making the "big decision" is a four-part process.

1. Deciding on a specific candidate
2. Informing the candidate
3. Negotiating the final terms of the call
4. Presenting the candidate as the nominee to the congregation

Deciding on the Candidate

The big decision you ultimately will make—choosing one candidate to nominate and present to your congregation—will be in reality a number of smaller decisions. The first decision each member made was to serve on the search committee. At this point in your process your committee can look back and see that it worked hard and made numerous decisions while developing criteria for candidates. You will have read pages of PIF papers, and prayed for patience more often than you will be able to remember. You celebrated some accomplishments along the way.

Now is the time to pay attention to what you have accomplished and established throughout your work.

Bunty Ketchum says that for a time a search team becomes a church within a church, a group of people gathered to discern how the Holy Spirit can work through them. Your "big decision" should come from your spiritual discernment, as a "sense of the group." How will you know you have found the right person? How does "discernment" work when it concerns such a weighty matter?

I agree with Danny Morris and Charles Olsen that discernment is a fragile process. Consensus as a human endeavor is susceptible to undue pressure from skillful management or preconceived opinions. The discerning group must remind itself that it is seeking to see and act from God's perspective. The sense of a search team may be expressed in different ways. As Morris and Olsen note, sometimes the Spirit of God settles on a group so visibly that the group immediately sees its decision with clarity. Other times discerners arrive at the group "sense of the meeting" only through much prayer, sharing of personal leadings, and inward struggle and transformation. God can be at work in as profound a way in this experience as in the first.

What if your team gets stalled and has broad disagreement? Talk through the issues that are preventing consensus. The way out is through the difficulty, not around it. Get all the questions and concerns of the group out on the table. If another conversation with a candidate is necessary, then arrange it. The issue that most frequently stalls a search committee is choosing between two, three, or four seemingly equal candidates. Theodore McConnell, a United Church of Christ conference pastor, discusses in his book *Finding a Pastor* a potential pitfall for search committees under the heading "The Exhaustion Cycle."

McConnell observes that most committees and churches have an innate time line, which may or may not correspond to an announced target date for reaching a decision. The time line has more to do with the dynamics, stamina, and pressures that develop within and act on the committee than with anything else. Once the committee goes beyond this often-unrecognized time, it enters a new phase, which usually is an erratic downward spiral. Things begin to fall apart or drift or become deadlocked. Although the process can be put back on the track in some cases, in others it will slip off again or be concluded with an uneasy compromise. The real danger of the exhaustion cycle is that once it begins it often leads to a bad decision. McConnell notes that the exhaustion cycle is most likely to set in when a committee is down the road in the process and interviewing candidates, and has difficulty either narrowing the field or choosing between two fine candidates.

Morris and Olsen note that consensus does not mean everyone in a group is at the same level of agreement. Someone on a search team may say, "I would not make him my first choice, if I were making the decision alone, but I feel good enough about the rest of the committee's support for him that I will not stand in the way." One dissenting perspective may not be a problem, but more than one can ultimately lead to dissent in the congregation if the dissenters choose to air their dissent publicly after the candidate is called and installed. Ideally, your decision should be unanimous and made with enthusiastic agreement.

As you prepare to make the decision, your presbytery COM liaison will help you dot the i's and cross the t's in the nominating procedures. Let's review that section of the *Book of Order* regarding your COM relationship (G.11.0502d):

> [The committee on ministry] shall counsel with churches regarding calls for permanent pastoral relations, visiting and counseling with every committee elected to nominate a pastor or associate pastor. It shall

advise with the committee regarding the merits, availability, and suitability of any candidate or minister
whose name is contemplated for nomination to the
congregation, and shall have the privilege of suggesting names to the committee. *No call to a permanent
pastoral relationship shall be in order for consideration by the presbytery unless the church has received
and considered the committee's counsel before action
is taken to issue a call.* (Emphasis added)

Some search teams have chosen to circumvent the
counsel of their presbytery COM. Don't make that decision. They are a part of your process to help, not hinder.

Informing the Candidate of Your Decision

This action should take place through a phone call and
should be the responsibility of your leader. The communication should be straightforward and to the point: "Our
committee is unanimous in its desire to present you as our
candidate to our congregation." Don't expect an immediate yes or no. But you may get either response. In most
cases, your candidate will need some time to think and
pray about her or his decision. Remember, candidates are
also working within a discernment process. What if your
invitation is rejected? The team leader should get a good
sense of what is being rejected. Is it the call itself? Your
candidate might be under consideration by another search
committee. The candidate could have concerns about the
compensation package and other terms. Remember, you
have rejected some candidates. Your number-one candidate may choose not to accept your call. Move on through
your short list of candidates. If you are having serious
problems with all the candidates you talk with and
become thoroughly stalled, then you should review the
qualifications you have set.

Negotiating the Final Terms of Call

Once your candidate has said yes, you are ready to finalize the terms of call. The same group of two or three members from your team who had the informal discussion with candidates about the terms and your compensation package should negotiate the terms of the call that will be presented to the presbytery. They should present your total package broken into its various parts. Whatever alterations you make to salary and housing as you finalize the terms of call will affect the amount of money necessary for pension and major medical compensation.

Presenting Your Nominee to the Congregation

Prepare a report for the congregation. Your report should include something of the process that your search team followed, including the number and kinds of PIFs reviewed, the criteria used, and the results of suggestions from members of the congregation. A brief biographical sketch and photograph of the candidate as a brochure or flyer will be of help in introducing your candidate to the congregation. The report can be mailed out in advance of the weekend the congregation will meet and vote on the candidate.

Let's accept the fact that we live in a less-trusting culture than thirty or forty years ago. One way to help your candidate begin to earn congregational trust is to plan some informal occasions for the candidate to meet the session, deacons, and support staff if yours is a large congregation, and then to meet members of the congregation.

Traditionally search committees introduced a candidate on a Sunday morning following what is termed the "candidating sermon." Here is a suggestion for an entire weekend. On Friday evening have an informal dinner for the candidate (and his or her family if applicable) with session members and members of the search team. Gather the deacons for a Saturday morning breakfast with the candidate. Then Saturday afternoon from 2 to 4 P.M. invite members of the congregation to an informal gathering to meet your candidate. This schedule requires a lot of socializing on the part of the candidate, but I have heard reports from candidates and search teams who said the procedure was a fine introduction to the current leaders of the congregation and the congregation itself. When the candidates began worship leadership on Sunday, they could look out and see a significant number of people they had met. They were not preaching to strangers.

Following the candidate's sermon there is an official congregational meeting, at which time the leader or leaders present the formal nomination. This presentation should not be hurried and stiff. Some additional background information can be presented by members of the search team. Some members of the congregation may want additional information or have questions. If you have done your work well, you will have no difficulty with questions or requests for additional information.

One final time: *Don't rush the process.* I know of a committee chairperson who did just that. The committee went through a weekend of introducing their candidate and came to Sunday and the time to present him for the vote of the congregation of about three hundred members. Two hundred were in worship that Sunday. When the search committee chair stood to present the candidate following worship, he made no preliminary comments and preempted the moderator of the congregational meeting by saying in a hurried and anxious voice, "We are now ready to present our candidate for your vote. All in favor say yes." He was so nervous he forgot a ballot was required. There were a large number of "yes" votes, but when he asked for the "no" votes there were at least twenty-five or thirty. He was stunned and bewildered, began to stammer, and said, "I suppose we need to count the votes." At that point a teenager stood up and said he voted no because he had not been allowed to ask a question. The moderator wisely suggested a time for some general discussion, and a few additional questions were asked. Ultimately a much more positive vote resulted. All but two of those who voted no said they would not have voted no had they been given a chance to ask questions or comment.

Chapter 8

Closure

As you looked at the title of this chapter, you may have asked yourself, "What does he mean by closure? Who needs closure? When you're done, you're done." Yes, but not exactly. When your congregation votes yes on the candidate your search team nominates, that ends your searching and nominating responsibilities. Closure essentially means putting the finishing touches on the whole process. You worked hard at getting started as a committee and throughout your search process. Now put some effort into ending your work. First, celebrate! Then, here are two recommendations.

Evaluate the Process

By all means, write a review of your work as a search team. This task may sound formal and arduous, but it shouldn't be. It can and should be fun and continue to feed your faith. This is not a job for one person. The whole team should be involved. Remember your day away, or retreat, at the beginning? Take another day away to do this wrap-up evaluation.

You will need a note taker. If you saved the newsprint from your CIF preparation, take it along.

Start your evaluation with the positive. What worked well and why? What do you think should be done next time the way you did it? What could have or should have been done differently? Let the stories flow, from the humorous accounts of travel experiences to sharing about meals. What about the time you showed up at the wrong church? Feel free to add to one another's comments.

In essence, leave a history of your work and life together for the next search team elected by your congregation. If every PNC or APNC in every church across the country had left such a history over the years, there would be no need for this book. There should be a file in every church office titled "PNC or APNC Evaluations." But let me hasten to add: your work should be understood as a self-evaluation and not a review of the committee's efforts by your session. Remember what I said at the outset. No one can put together in concise form the principles, rules, and directions needed for mastery of the task of calling new pastoral leadership. The task must have some fluidity and flexibility. What worked well ten years ago may not work well now, and what worked well for you may not work well ten years in the future. Your evaluation and review of your work ought to be understood as "how it was done once" not "how it should always be done."

In writing this book, I have discovered that a number of churches do have these evaluations or reviews. Take a look in the church files and ask around in your congregation to see if there is some PNC or APNC history for you to review.

Serve as a Transition Team
for the New Pastor or Associate Pastor

The end of your search will mark the beginning of the work of the pastor or associate pastor your congregation called. Your session may choose to put together a transition team. If they do not, my second recommendation (and it will require some additional work on your part) is for your search team to become a transition team.

Think about this concept and talk it over before acting on it. A support group is a fine idea if everybody is in agreement, and I mean everybody. The key player is your new pastor or associate pastor. I think most pastors will welcome the idea of a support team and in fact will ask for such a group. However, a support group or transition team is not a concept to force on anyone just because you think it's a great idea. *How* you go about your support is the crucial factor.

What Should a Support Group or Transition Team Do?

Your support group or transition team, regardless of the name, should not be, or act like, a personnel committee. Nor should this group of people look like a "clique" of your new pastor's close friends. This team is not an "insiders" group. The primary work of the transition team will be to assist your new pastor or associate pastor and her or his family with their move into the church community and into the larger community. Your assistance should begin with making sure that all the arrangements agreed upon in negotiating the call have been carried out or are in the right hands. The arrangements will have to do with such items as moving date, finances, and home and office improvements.

One committee I know took on this work at the invitation of their new pastor. He arrived with his family in May. The former search team, with the blessing of session, agreed to meet with him and his wife once a month. These were usually brief times with a lot of emphasis on positive feedback and occasionally some gentle negative feedback. The pastor asked for the latter so he could hear some constructive commentary early. The team worked to avoid the "picky gossip" that is inevitable. They had prepared, in advance, a booklet with information about physicians, dentists, plumbers, and food shopping, and took time in their monthly gatherings to discuss these matters and any other questions, such as the adjustment of the children to the church and community. There was also an emphasis on fun in each gathering. These meetings continued over the summer and through November. At the November gathering there was agreement that the meetings had been very fruitful but it was not necessary to continue them.

Tell the above story to your new pastor or associate pastor and see if he or she wants to consider a six- to nine-month support relationship. You can be of great help with your new pastor's or associate pastor's transition into the community and into the life of your church. You can also serve as a sounding board for the honeymoon and shakedown period. Roy Oswald, author of the Alban Institute's publication *The Pastor as Newcomer,* gives some good counsel about a pastor's transition into the life of a congregation and community. Getting settled in a new home and finding one's way around a new congregation can be exhausting and frustrating. Sometimes the "settling in" phase involves first-time home ownership for a pastor or associate pastor. That experience can be unsettling, especially if a candidate has never seen a utility bill and then receives a gas and electric bill of $370 for the first month.

Another issue for new pastoral leaders that Oswald notes is getting even more deeply acquainted with a congregation's history. Good candidates will probe for that history in their interviews with you. All congregations, except new church developments, have stories about days of glory, remembered and forgotten crises, and times of turmoil. Look for ways to help your new pastor or associate pastor learn some of your congregation's stories. Talk about some of the "customs" of your congregation, especially those regarding worship. The quickest way for a new pastor to get in trouble is to tinker with the worship service, either knowingly or unknowingly.

A recent seminary graduate arrived at church one morning to celebrate his first baptism, early in his new call as pastor. He found a rosebud in a vase near the pulpit. Assuming someone had left it there by mistake, he took it to his study, intending to ask about it after the service. He later discovered that presenting a rose to the parents of each baptized baby was part of a long-standing tradition in the congregation, and it took him about six months to smooth the ruffled feathers of some deacons. The interim pastor had refused to present the rosebud, saying it had nothing to do with the sacrament of Baptism. The deacons believed the interim had passed along his perspective to the new pastor.

You cannot eliminate all such surprises for your new pastor or associate pastor, but you can help in clarifying the expectations and sometimes assist in renegotiating them. Some church leadership specialists argue that no one arrives as "pastor," but slowly over time becomes pastor, and that the "becoming" is a three- to five-year process.

You have finished reading. Now it is time to begin the search work.

Appendix A

Important *Book of Order* Procedures for a PNC or APNC

G-14.0502 Election of a Pastor

Elect a Pastor Nominating Committee

a. When a church is without a pastor, or after the effective date of the dissolution of the pastoral relationship, the congregation shall, with the guidance and permission of the committee on ministry, G-11.0502d, proceed to elect a pastor in the following manner. The session shall call a congregational meeting to elect a nominating committee, which shall be representative of the whole congregation. This committee's duty shall be to nominate a minister to the congregation for election as pastor. Public notice of the time, place, and purpose of the meeting shall be given at least ten days in advance, which shall include two successive Sundays.

Work of the Committee

b. The nominating committee shall confer with the committee on ministry as provided in G-11.0502d and when seeking an associate pastor or co-pastor, with the pastor or any continuing co-pastors. Care must be taken to consider candidates without regard to race, ethnic origin, sex, marital status, age or disabilities.

Report of the Committee

c. When the committee is ready to report, it shall notify the session, which shall call a congregational meeting, giving public notice as required in the paragraph a. above, for the purpose of acting on the report of the nominating committee. The same procedure shall be followed in the selection of an associate pastor. The action of the congregation, if favorable, shall be presented to the presbytery for its concurrence. If the presbytery concurs, it shall make arrangements for the minister's installation. A call to a permanent pastoral relationship shall not be issued until it has been approved by the presbytery. (G-11.0502d)

G-14.0503 Congregational Meeting

Convened for Election of Pastor

a. When a congregation is convened for the election of a pastor (associate pastor), the moderator of the session appointed by presbytery or some other minister of the presbytery shall preside.

Vote by Ballot

b. Following prayer for the guidance of God, the moderator shall call for the report of the nominating committee. Following the report, the moderator shall then put the question: "Are you ready to proceed to the election of a pastor (associate pastor)?" If they are ready the moderator shall declare the name submitted by the nominating committee to be in nomination. The vote shall be upon the question whether the congregation, under the will of God, shall call the person nominated to be its pastor (associate pastor), and it shall be taken by ballot. In every case a majority of the voters present and voting shall be required to elect.

G-14.0504 Larger Parish

When two or more churches established by presbytery as a larger parish unite in calling a pastor, the call must specify the support promised by each church. With the approval of presbytery, such a call may be issued by a larger parish council providing for the approval of the churches given in properly called meetings of their congregations, for payment of a total salary from a common parish treasury along with an explanation of the financial agreement between the churches of the parish, and for the annual review of the pastor's salary by the parish council with provision for a vote thereon by each congregation. When such a call has been issued by a parish council, and approved by the presbytery, each participating church shall be obligated to continue its financial support of the parish for the duration of the pastorate, unless excused by the other participating churches with the approval of the presbytery. The call shall specify that the minister is called to be pastor (associate pastor) of the churches constituting the parish.

G-14.0505 Dissent

On the election of a pastor (associate pastor), if it appears that a substantial minority of the voters are averse to the nominee who has received a majority of the votes, and that they cannot be persuaded to concur in the call, the moderator shall recommend to the majority that they not prosecute the call. If the congregation is nearly unanimous, or if the majority insist upon their right to call a pastor (associate pastor), the moderator shall forward the call to the presbytery, certifying the number of those who do not concur in the call and any other facts of importance. The moderator shall also inform the person being called of the nature and circumstances of the decision.

G-14.0506 The Call

Persons Elected to Sign the Call

a. Persons shall be elected by the vote of the congregation to sign the call and to present and prosecute the call before the presbytery. The moderator of the meeting shall certify to the presbytery that those signing the call were properly elected and that the call was in all other respects prepared as constitutionally required.

Form

b. The call shall be in the following or like form:

The _____ Presbyterian Church (U.S.A.) of (Location) _____ belonging to _____ Presbytery, being well satisfied with your qualifications for ministry and confident that we have been led to you by the Holy Spirit as one whose service will be profitable to the spiritual interest of our church and fruitful for the Kingdom of our Lord, earnestly and solemnly calls you, (Name) _____, to undertake the office of pastor (or associate pastor) of this congregation, promising you in the discharge of your duty all proper support, encouragement, and allegiance in the Lord.

That you may be free to devote yourself full time (part time) to the ministry of the Word and Sacrament among us, we promise and obligate ourselves to pay the following (those agreed upon are to be filled in):

Annual salary
 (in regular monthly payments) .. $_____
Use of the manse .... $_____
Housing allowance .... $_____
Utilities allowance .... $_____
Other medical insurance .... $_____
Professional expenses
 Automobile expenses .... $_____
 Continuing education expenses .. $_____
 Book expenses .... $_____
 Personal business expenses ..... $_____
 Other (specify) .... $_____
Moving costs .... $_____
Vacation of (time period) .... _____
Continuing Education (time period) _____

And we will pay regularly in advance to the board responsible for benefits a sum equal to that requisite percent of your salary which may be fixed by the General Assembly of the Presbyterian Church (U.S.A.) for participation in the Benefits Plan of the Presbyterian Church (U.S.A.), including both pension and medical coverage, or any successor plan approved by the General Assembly, during the time of your being and continuing in the pastoral relationship set forth in this call to this church. We further promise and obligate ourselves to review with you annually the adequacy of this compensation. In testimony whereof we have subscribed our names this _____ day of _____, A.D. _____.

(Signatures)

Allowances and Amounts

c. The call shall specify all and only those allowances and amounts which are undertaken as part of the call. If the minister is obligated to fulfill military commitments during a period of pastoral service, an agreement between the minister and the calling agency may be added to the terms of call for that obligation and potential mobilization of the minister, and become an element in the terms of call when approved by presbytery. If the call is for less than full time, the precise terms of the contract shall be indicated.

Certification

d. The certification by the moderator shall be as follows:

> Having moderated the congregational meeting which extended a call to (Name)_____ for ministerial services, I do certify that the call has been made in all respects according to the rules laid down in the Form of Government, and that the persons who signed the foregoing call were authorized to do so by vote of the _____ Presbyterian Church (U.S.A.).
>
> (Signed)_____
> Moderator of the Meeting

Minimum Requirements

e. The terms of the call shall always provide for compensation that meets or exceeds any minimum requirements of the presbytery in effect when the call is made and shall thereafter be adjusted annually as required to conform to such requirement.

Integration

f. Every call to a candidate shall be accompanied by a description of the presbytery's plan for the integration of new ministers into the life and work of presbytery. (G-11.0103n)

G-14.0507 Call Presented and Received

Presbytery Finds Call in Order

a. If the presbytery finds the call in order and determines that it is for the good of the whole church, it shall inform the person being called of its decision and shall proceed to present the call through the presbytery having jurisdiction over the minister or candidate.

Call through Own Presbytery

b. No minister or candidate shall receive a call except through the hands of his or her own presbytery. When a church in one presbytery extends a call to a minister or candidate of another presbytery, the stated clerk of the calling presbytery shall transmit the call to the stated clerk of the other presbytery, with certification that the call has been found in order by the presbytery. The stated clerk of the minister's or candidate's presbytery shall deliver the call to the committee on ministry (G-11.0502b), which shall inform the presbytery of the receipt of the call and shall recommend to presbytery what action should be taken with respect to it. If the presbytery thinks it wise to release the minister from the present charge, it may present the call to her or him with permission to transfer to the presbytery having jurisdiction over the church, there to be examined and received. If the presbytery thinks it wise for the candidate to accept the call, it may present the call to her or him with the permission to be examined by the presbytery having jurisdiction over the church. If the examination is not sustained, the minister or candidate remains under the jurisdiction of his or her own presbytery. The presbyteries shall deal directly with each other through their stated clerks in certifying both the call of the church and the credentials of the minister or candidate.

G-11.0500 Committee on Ministry

G-11.0501 Nature and Membership

c. Each presbytery shall elect a committee on ministry to serve as pastor and counselor to the ministers of the presbytery, to facilitate the relations between congregations, ministers, and the presbytery, and to settle difficulties on behalf of presbytery when possible and expedient.

G-11.0502 Responsibilities

d. [The committee] shall counsel with churches regarding calls for permanent pastoral relations, visiting and counseling with every committee elected to nominate a pastor or associate pastor. It shall advise with the committee regarding the merits, availability, and suitability of any candidate or minister whose name is contemplated for nomination to the congregation, and shall have the privilege of suggesting names to the committee. No call to a permanent pastoral relationship shall be in order for consideration by the presbytery unless the church has received and considered the committee's counsel before action is taken to issue a call.

Appendix B

Sample Congregational Reports and Action Plan

These reports and the action plan were developed by the PNC of the First Presbyterian Church of Arlington Heights, Illinois, and are included as examples of what can be done in effective planning and reporting:

November 1996

The Pastor Nominating Committee (PNC) was elected on October 15 and began work immediately—five meetings so far! Like all of you, the members of the PNC are excited about the prospect of calling a new pastor, anxious to get it done quickly, and, quickly or not, determined to do the very best job possible. To keep you posted, the PNC will report progress on a regular basis—monthly, if at all possible. This is the first report.

A three-stage process has been defined by the PNC for completing the pastoral search. This is shown in the diagram on the reverse side of this page. The three stages can be summarized as: (1) establish our requirements for the position of senior pastor; (2) conduct a broad and thorough search, screening the responses to a final set of candidates; and (3) evaluate the candidates and make a selection.

At this point the PNC is deep into Stage 1, defining our requirements. The product of this stage will be a completed Church Information Form (CIF)—the standard (and required) form used by the PC(USA) for describing a church, documenting the leadership qualifications of the pastor it is seeking, and outlining the job description and terms of the call. The CIF must be approved by the session and the committee on ministry of the Presbytery of Chicago before it can be sent to candidates. The PNC hopes to complete the Church Information Form by January. We are interested in your input so please call any of the people below with comments!

Tom Carroll	Cindy Koerner	Jim Mayer
Jennifer Fick	Mary Krigas	Joyce Millner
Bill Ginnodo	Lynn Kunz	Courtney Munz
John Gmitro, Chair	Rob Lincoln	Dick Reeves
Jane Harris	Laura Liston	Bob Winter

(On the reverse side of each report was the following three-stage reporting system.)

The work of the PNC is being done in three stages, indicated below by the large boxes. Each stage has several tasks, which are listed below the stages.

Stage 1	Stage 2	Stage 3
Preliminary Stage Establish Requirements	Main Stage Conduct Broad Search	Final Stage Interview & Reach Consensus

✓Establish plan, budget, and scope.	• Determine and contact sources	• Interview the final set of candidates
✓Assemble basic information	• Develop screening process	• Evaluate; identify the candidate of choice
❖Document needs & wants	• Evaluate responses	• Obtain Presbytery, Session and Congregation approval

• Write the job description and
Complete the PC(USA)
Church Information Form

• Make preliminary visits/calls

• Document PNC processes

• Obtain approval of Session
and Presbytery

• Screen to final set of limited
size

**The symbols in front of the tasks show where we are in the
process as of today:**
✓ This step is done
❖ We're working on this step
• Yet to be done

May 17, 1997

For our May report, we would like to tell you about the
process we are using to evaluate candidates. It has four
steps:

1 Evaluate dossiers. Candidates who apply to us for the
position of Pastor/Head of Staff provide us with a dossier
known as a Personal Information Form. The "PIF" is a
standard document of the PC(USA) that describes a pastor's training, skills, and job history. We screen these
carefully to identify candidates who, on paper at least,
meet our requirements.

2 ❖Conduct telephone interview. Candidates whose PIF
passes our test are called and interviewed by a team of
PNC members. The telephone interview further explores
a candidate's characteristics, viewpoints, and qualifications.

3 • Visit candidates' churches. Selected candidates will be
visited in their home churches to observe preaching skills
and to seek evidence of the working of the Spirit.

4 • Visits to us. Final candidates will be invited to spend
a weekend with us to view the church and community,
preach in a neutral pulpit, and participate in an in-depth
interview with the full PNC.

To date we have received a total of 75 dossiers. We have just about finished evaluating them, and are now beginning the telephone interviews. It is exciting to be this far! Please keep us in your prayers as we continue the evaluation process, and please feel free to call any one of us at any time with your recommendations, comments, or suggestions.

Tom Carroll	Cindy Koerner	Jim Mayer
Jennifer Fick	Mary Krigas	Joyce Millner
Bill Ginnodo	Lynn Kunz	Courtney Munz
John Gmitro, Chair	Rob Lincoln	Dick Reeves
Jane Harris	Laura Liston	Bob Winter

Appendix C

Soul Food: Readings and Hymns to Guide and Sustain Your Work

Genesis 1:1–2:4

Genesis 12:1–9

Genesis 18:13–15

Genesis 28:10–22

Exodus (Read often from this entire book, both alone and as a committee. It is filled with soul food, but especially the following texts: 3:1–15; 6:2–9; 15:1–18; 18:13–23; 20:1–17; 33; 40:34–38)

Deuteronomy 4:32–40; 6:1–9; 8; 34

Joshua 24

Ruth

1 Samuel 1:1–20; 3:1–18; 8; 16:1–13

2 Samuel 7; 12:1–25

1 Kings 3; 19:1–18

Read frequently from the Psalms, especially 1; 8; 16; 19; 23; 24; 25; 34; 42; 46; 51; 67; 90; 91; 95; 96; 100; 103; 121; 130; and 139

Ecclesiastes 3:1–15

Isaiah 35; 43; 45; 48

Matthew 5:1–7:28; 9:10–17; 11:1–24; 14:13–21; 18:21–35; 20:1–16

Mark 2:1–12; 3:13–19; 6:1–13; 10:32–45; 14:26-31

Luke 1:26–38; 4:1–30; 6:17–49; 8:4–15; 9:51–62; 10:29–37; 12:13–21; 24:13–35

John 1:1–18; 2:13–22; 3:1–21; 4:1–42; 9; 16; 17
Acts 1:12–26; 5:12–42; 6:1–7; 8:26–39; 9:1–22; 10;
    15:1–35; 17:16–34
Romans 5:1–5; 8:31–39; 12:1–2
1 Corinthians 1:10–31; 3:10–23; 12:1–13:13
Ephesians 4:1–16
Philippians 2:1–18; 4:4–7
1 Peter 2:1–10

Your hymnal is a rich source of soul food. Consider
using these various hymns from time to time. (The num-
bers are from *The Presbyterian Hymnal,* 1990.)

"Come, Thou Long-Expected Jesus," #1 or #2; use in
    Advent. You have the option of two fine tunes.
"Be Thou My Vision," #339
"For the Beauty of the Earth," #473
"All People That on Earth Do Dwell," #220
"Let All Things Now Living," # 554
"Lord, Dismiss Us with Thy Blessing," #538
"Come, Christians, Join to Sing," #150
"We Gather Together," #559
"Live into Hope," #332
"In Christ There Is No East or West," #439 or #440
"Blest Be the Tie That Binds," #438
"I Sing a Song of the Saints of God," #364
"Beneath the Cross of Jesus," #92
"Go to Dark Gethsemane," #97
"God of the Sparrow," #272
"Let Us with a Gladsome Mind," #244
"My Shepherd Will Supply My Need," #172
"The Church's One Foundation," #442
"We Give Thee but Thine Own," #428
"Joyful, Joyful, We Adore Thee," #464

Appendix D

Sample Congregational Survey

1. List in order of importance to you five characteristics and qualities you want our new pastor or associate pastor to have.

2. What has caused you greatest concern about our church?

3. What one aspect about our church would you never want to see changed?

4. What about our church would you like to see changed as soon as possible?

Feel free to offer comments about your experience in the life of this congregation and any other information you would like the PNC/APNC to know.

Appendix E

Sample Acknowledgment and Rejection Letters

Acknowledgment letter sent within one week of receiving a PIF from a candidate as a self-referral:

Dear _____ :

　　Thank you for your recent letter and PIF for the position of _____ at _____ Church of _____.

　　The PNC/APNC is in the process of reviewing materials we have received, and will be in touch with you at a later date. Thank you for your interest in our church.

Sincerely,

Rejection letter for candidates who do not meet your mandatory criteria. Send as soon as decision has been made—four weeks at the earliest, six weeks at the latest:

Dear _____ :

　　Thank you for your interest in the position of _____ at _____ Church of _____, and for submitting your PIF. The

PNC/APNC has been impressed by the many fine candidates who have indicated an interest in this position.

Your PIF (and other materials) have been carefully studied by our committee in the light of our current needs. We have determined that there is not a sufficient correspondence between your goals and qualifications and our pastoral position as we have defined it.

The committee joins me in praying for God's blessing on your present and future ministry and in asking for your prayers as we seek new leadership.

Sincerely,

Appendix F

Basic Types of Interview Questions

Open Questions—"Tell us a little about yourself."

Open questions are broad and basically unstructured. They indicate the topic to be discussed and allow whoever is answering the question to structure the answer. "How would you describe yourself?" A candidate might ask, "How would you describe this congregation?"

Open questions can be used:

To establish rapport

To learn about attitudes, feelings, frames of reference

Direct Questions—"How many hours do you spend in sermon preparation?"

Direct questions ask for explanation or expansion of a particular point. "What is your strongest ministry skill?" A candidate might ask, "What one aspect of this congregation would you never want to see change?"

Direct questions can be used:

To get a specific reply on a specific topic

May be phrased indirectly to lessen threat: "I wonder how many hours you usually spend in preparing your sermons?"

Closed Questions—"Do you see your gifts as strongest in preaching, teaching, or pastoral care?"

Closed questions are like direct questions, but they narrow the possible range of responses. Closed questions are useful:

> When you want to classify or get agreement or disagreement with a particular viewpoint
> When used with a limited number of frames of reference
> When information sought is not threatening

Yes or No Questions—"Do you preach longer than twenty-five minutes?"

Yes or no questions are an extreme form of the closed question, which generally allows only a yes or no answer. These questions usually do not get much information and often resemble the "third degree." "Will you stay here longer than three years?" "Do you expect to have children in the near future?" (This is not only an inappropriate question, it is illegal.) Or a candidate might ask, "Will the congregation support my ministry?" Neither of these approaches will get any helpful information. Yes/no questions are by and large to be avoided.

Probe Questions—"I would welcome hearing more of your thinking about emphasizing financial stewardship year-round."

Probe questions are helpful when used to stimulate discussion and obtain further information or an elaboration. They invite clarification, enlargement, explanation, and deeper responses. "Tell us more about preaching on controversial subjects."

Appendix G

Sample Evaluation Form for a Church Visit

Name of Minister _____ Date Heard _____

Present Location _____

Rating (Write in your choice—5 is high)   5 4 3 2 1

1. Appearance & Manner (presence in pulpit)
2. Order of Worship
3. Quality of Worship Material
4. Conduct of Service
   a. voice, language used
   b. poise/mannerisms
   c. relationship with others: in pulpit; with organist
5. Sermon
   Method of delivery (notes? read? memorized?)
   Fill Out Sermon Evaluation Form
6. Relationship with Congregation
   a. during service
   b. as met at door
   c. general atmosphere in church
7. Personality Impression
8. Can you see this person in our pulpit?
9. Will he/she wear well?
10. Other Comments:

Your Name:

Appendix H

Sample Sermon Evaluation Forms

Form # 1:

Pastor's Name _____ Sermon Date _____
Sermon Title _____ Audio___ Video___ Live___
Overall Score (1–5 highest)___ Length in Time____
Elements of sermon evaluated on a 5 pt. scale (1–5 highest)   5 4 3 2 1

DELIVERY

1. Voice (warm, natural, clear diction)
2. Shared discovery (teaching/explaining vs. confrontational—"gospel according to me")
3. Use of humor/anecdotes/stories
4. Personal conviction/passion/emotion
5. Appeal—Was I urged to do anything?

SERMON

1. Theology: connection to scripture and rest of service
2. Development and logical conclusion
3. Relevance to daily life (church, world, me)
4. Evidence of personal thought/reading/scholarship
5. Can you remember main points of sermon? (Will they be remembered a week from now?)

Subjective considerations: "Preaching will fill the church"; other considerations:

Form # 2:

Candidate:_____ Date:_____

Evaluator:_____

Sermon Title:_____

Scripture:_____

Subject (Express in one sentence the central thought of the sermon):

_____

_____

Rating Scale: 5 (Excellent) 4 (Very Good) 3 (Average)
              2 (Below Average) 1 (Poor)

I. CONTENT

   A. *Design and Organization*

   1. Introduction (short; accurate; grabbed attention)
____

   2. Progression (good movement from point to point)
____

   3. Conclusion (concise; creative; motivating) ____

   4. Clarity (easy to follow and understand) ____

   5. Overall organization (well assembled as a whole)
____

                                Subtotal _____

   B. *Message*

   1. Use of Scripture (relevant connection between scripture and message) ____

   2. Relevance (addressed current issues and concerns of both individuals and larger society; appropriate to occasion) ____

   3. Theological Integrity (based in Reformed theology; true to the gospel) ____

4. Theme (central message clearly and precisely stated) ____
5. Intellectual Integrity (well reasoned, creative, and thorough analysis, thought provoking for congregation ____
6. Interest (held congregation's attention; enjoyable) ____
7. Impact (worth the congregation's time; important to the pastor; congregation motivated to act) ____
8. Lift (congregation moved on an emotional level by certain passage or phrase)____

Subtotal _____

II. DELIVERY

1. Poise (at ease, confident demeanor)____
2. Eye Contact (made and sustained eye contact with entire congregation; appropriate use of notes) ____
3. Voice (volume, voice quality, appropriate variations in volume, rate, pitch, inflections)____
4. Body (appropriate use of gestures and movement; no distracting habits) ____
5. Eloquence (thoroughly familiar and comfortable with message; good choice of words; effective use of metaphors, quotations, examples, humor to convey message) ____
6. Mistakes (misstatements, mispronunciations, loss of place or train of thought) ____
7. Length (appropriate to message and place within overall worship service)____

Subtotal _____

III. NOTES AND COMMENTS

IV. OVERALL RATING (20 to 100)   _____
Should the PNC consider this candidate further?

No _____

Yes _____

Appendix I

Questions a Candidate May Ask

General Question
Why am I of interest to you as a candidate?

Nature of the Congregation
Tell me about the history of the congregation. What have been some of the high points and some of the disappointments?

What are the major strengths of your congregation? the weaknesses?

What are the three greatest challenges in your church that the next pastor will have to face?

Worship Life
How would you describe your worship?

What aspect of your worship would you never want to see changed? What aspect of your worship would you like to change as soon as possible?

How are decisions about baptisms made?

How does your congregation define "biblical preaching"?

Outreach
How is your congregation committed to a ministry in the community?

How does your community view your church?

What role would you like your pastor to take in community service organizations and ecumenical activities?

Program

In a few words, what would you say is the mission of your congregation?

How was that mission determined, and is it written down somewhere?

How does your congregation set goals and priorities?

Finances

How does this congregation go about building budgets?

What is the present financial condition of the congregation?

What part do you expect your pastor to take in financial stewardship?

Denominational Commitment

In what ways does your congregation relate to the governing bodies of the PC(USA) and the programs of the denomination?

How does presbytery view your congregation?

Bibliography

Achtemeier, Elizabeth. *So You're Looking for a New Preacher.* Grand Rapids: Wm. B. Eerdmans, 1991.

Bratcher, Ed, Robert Kemper, and Douglas Scott. *Mastering Transitions.* Portland, Oreg.: Multnomah, 1991.

Brown, William C. *Training a Pastor Nominating Committee in the Search for a Compatible Pastor.* Ann Arbor: University of Michigan Press, 1991.

Carroll, Jackson W., Carl S. Dudley, and William McKinney, eds. *Handbook for Congregational Studies.* Nashville: Abingdon Press, 1986.

Dean, Kenda Creasy, and Ron Foster. *The Godbearing Life: The Art of Soul-Tending for Youth Ministry.* Nashville: Upper Room, 1998.

Dingman, Robert. *In Search of a Leader: The Complete Search Committee Guidebook.* Westlake Village, Calif.: Lakeside Books, 1994.

Farnham, Suzanne G., Joseph P. Gill, R. Taylor McLean, and Susan M. Ward. *Listening Hearts.* Harrisburg, Pa.: Morehouse Publishing Co., 1991.

Fletcher, John C. *Religious Authenticity in the Clergy.* Washington, D.C.: The Alban Institute, 1989.

Half, Robert. *The Robert Half Way to Get Hired in Today's Job Market.* New York: Rawson Wade Publishers, 1981.

Hobgood, William Chris. *The Once and Future Pastor.* Washington, D.C.: The Alban Institute, 1998.

Hopewell, James. *Congregation: Stories and Structure.* Edited by Barbara Wheeler. Philadelphia: Fortress Press, 1987.

Ketchum, Bunty. *So You're on the Search Committee.* Washington, D.C.: The Alban Institute, 1985.

McConnell, Theodore A. *Finding a Pastor.* Minneapolis: Winston Press, 1986.

Morris, Danny, and Charles Olsen. *Discerning God's Will Together: A Spiritual Practice for the Church.* Nashville: Upper Room, 1997.

Olsen, Charles M. *Transforming Church Boards into Communities of Spiritual Leaders.* Washington, D.C.: The Alban Institute, 1995.

Oswald, Roy. *The Pastor as Newcomer.* Washington, D.C.: The Alban Institute, 1990.

Parsons, George, and Speed Leas. *Understanding Your Congregation as a System.* Washington, D.C.: The Alban Institute, 1993.

Rebeck, Victoria A. "Gifted for Ministry: Setting Up Pastors for Success." *Christian Century* (June 30–July 7, 1993): 670–75.

Scheer, Wilbert E. *Personnel Administration Handbook.* Chicago: Dartnell Press, 1979.

Stevens, R. Paul, and Phil Collins. *The Equipping Pastor: A Systems Approach to Congregational Leadership.* Washington, D.C.: The Alban Institute, 1993.

Stewart, Charles J., and William B. Cash. *Interviewing: Principles and Practices.* 5th ed. Dubuque, Iowa: William C. Brown, 1988.

White, Edward. "What Kind of Pastor Will Most Likely Empower Laity?" *Congregations: The Alban Journal* (May/June 1994): 12–13.

CPSIA information can be obtained at www.ICGtesting.com
Printed in the USA
LVOW090344270612

287776LV00001B/27/P